To Margaret, 05/11
Jeff's me_____
Celebr_____.

Oh Brother!

THE LIFE & TIMES OF **JEFF FAZZOLARI**

Cliff Fazzolari

CLIFF FAZZOLARI

SterlingHouse
Publisher, Inc.

Pittsburgh, PA

ISBN-10: 1-58501-158-4
ISBN-13: 978-1-58-501158-2
Trade Paperback
© Copyright 2011 Cliff Fazzolari
All Rights Reserved
Library of Congress #2010927248

Requests for information should be addressed to:
SterlingHouse Publisher, Inc.
3468 Babcock Boulevard
Pittsburgh, PA 15237
info@sterlinghousepublisher.com
www.sterlinghousepublisher.com

SterlingHouse Books
is an imprint of SterlingHouse Publisher, Inc.

Cover Design: Nicole M. Tibbitt
Interior Design: Jessica A. Hilderbrand

Printed in Canada

"To laugh often and much; to win the respect of intelligent people and the affection of children; to earn the appreciation of honest critics and endure the betrayal of false friends; to appreciate beauty; to find the best in others; to leave the world a little better than we found it, whether by a healthy child, a garden patch or a redeemed social condition; to know even one life breathed easier because you lived. This is to have succeeded."

- Anonymous

Dedication

This book is dedicated to Johnny, Rocco and Farrah. May the love of your Dad ring true to your hearts for every single day of your lives.

Chapter I – Tomorrow Never Knows

January 27, 2009   There is a time for everything, and a season for every activity under heaven. A time to weep and a time to laugh, a time to mourn and a time to dance. ECCL 3:1,4

It really should have been a great day for the Fazzolari family. The new Springsteen CD, Working on a Dream, was about to be released to the public, and as a group we were more than ready for it.

"It's like Christmas morning," I told my wife, Kathy, as I took the stairs two at a time. I kissed Kathy quickly, rubbed the heads of my boys, Matt, Jake and Sam, and chided them a bit.

"The 'god of music' has a new album out," I announced.

"They don't call them albums any more," Matthew said, "and besides, he's old."

I wasn't about to be deterred. I knew of a few people who were just as excited as me. My brothers John, Jim and Jeff and my sister Carrie and John's wife, Dana, were bound to be just as fired up. In fact, before the outside air even had the chance to settle into my bones, my cell phone vibrated. I knew it was Jeff calling before I even glanced down at the screen.

"Yo!" Jeff said. "What time does Target open?"

"Usually nine," I said, "but sometimes they don't get the new releases until ten."

"I'll be there at eight fifty-nine," Jeff said.

"I told Kathy that this is like Christmas morning," I answered.

Jeff laughed. "I know, I told Lynn that it was going to be the best day of the year, by far. Pretty lousy when you're only in January and you've already hit the best possible day."

"All right, call me when you've heard it," I said.

The telephone line went dead in my ear, and it wasn't much of a surprise. Jeff was the one sibling that I spoke with each and every day, and in a move that sometimes infuriated me, he always hung up before saying good-bye.

My job took me out of my home to construction sites all across western and central New York. It was one day when I was excited to be in the car, just driving and listening to the music. After visiting one site, I pulled into the lot at Target just a few minutes before nine a.m. The day was crisp and clear, but the low-hanging clouds didn't seem to be offering much of a threat of snow. It was a perfect day for the new Springsteen album.

I sat in the car in the store parking lot and opened the CD with hands that were close to shaking. The musical journey that Springsteen had taken us on since the late 1970s was an epic adventure. As a close-knit family, we had attended the concerts, sang the songs at each other's weddings and argued about the meaning of the lyrics.

Yet work beckoned and I traveled alone along I-90 between Buffalo and Dunkirk, visiting a number of clients along the way. It was turning out to be a wonderful day as the sounds of the new songs filled my truck, over and over.

My final stop was in the Silver Creek area. My plan was to visit the job and drive home to my office, where I'd write a few of the reports due before the start of the next day. My cell phone vibrated in my pocket just as I was getting out of the car, and I wasn't surprised to see the name 'Jeff' flashing on the screen.

"Hey, what do you think?" he asked.

"It's great," I said. "I've already listened to it a couple of times."

"I only got through the first four songs," Jeff responded. "But I'm going to eat a sandwich as big as your head and go into my office to listen to it. At the very least we have Outlaw Pete to listen to for the next thirty years."

I figured that Jeff just might hang up the phone right there, but he had a couple of other things on his mind.

"I got us a bunch of football squares for the Super Bowl. You owe me ten bucks, and the side of beef we ordered will be in by the end of March. Did I tell you that already?"

"Yeah, you did," I said.

"I just want to give you enough time to figure out how you're going to get out of picking it up," he said.

"You already said that, too," I muttered.

This time the line did go dead. Couldn't he have said good-bye just once?

Just twenty minutes later, as I was listening to the song Tomorrow Never Knows, my wife's call came through.

"They just rushed your brother to the hospital," she said.

"Which brother? Why?" I asked. It seemed as if my heart skipped a beat as the urgency in Kathy's voice sent a shiver of fear through my body.

"Jeff," Kathy said. "He collapsed at work. They took him to Mercy by ambulance."

It felt as if all the air had been sucked out of my lungs. "I...I just talked to him," I said. "He's fine."

"I'm telling you, Lynn called. I don't know what's going on."

"Did he faint?"

"That's all I know," Kathy said.

A wave of sheer panic took control of my movements, but I told myself that I'd be able to handle emergency mode. I was less than five minutes from the hospital, so I didn't bother to call anyone because I really didn't have anything to say. I just needed to see Jeff and find out for myself that everything was all right.

Everything had to be all right.

Lynn was pulling onto the parking ramp beside the hospital just as I was walking to the exit from the ramp. She rolled down the driver's side window and looked at me. "What's going on?" I asked.

"I don't know," she said softly. "What could it be?" In her eyes I saw terror and undeniable fear. I also saw a look that would be reflected back to me time and time again in the coming days. It was a look of resolve and love.

"He'll be okay," I said. "I'll wait for you."

Lynn parked and we hustled into the emergency room. Jeff was positioned behind a curtain, seated in a wheelchair. His eyelids were drooping and I had no way of knowing for sure, but his posture told me that there was something very wrong. But it wasn't as bad as it seemed, was it?

"Are you okay?" I asked. His eyes were clouded, but he heard my question and offered a thumbs-up.

Despite Jeff's upbeat signal to me, the staff was in full emergency mode. "He's had a brain bleed," someone said.

I thought of a co-worker who'd suffered an aneurysm. He'd been okay after a time. Someone else mentioned a stroke. A stroke? Didn't that happen to old people? A thirty-eight-year-old man didn't have a stroke, did he?

Lynn asked Jeff to move his arms and legs and he immediately responded to each request. That was good news, wasn't it?

"We need to take Jeff for tests that will assess the damage," the nurse announced.

Damage? To our brother? Our best friend in the world?

A great dad and husband? A terrific son?

"He's going to be all right?" I asked the nurse who happened to be passing by.

I didn't get an answer.

My vibrating cell phone was driving me absolutely crazy, but I didn't immediately answer any of the calls. I just kept drifting back into the room where Jeff was seated, and I couldn't help but wonder why the staff wasn't moving faster. If the situation were as serious as it seemed, wouldn't it pay to get to work on him right away?

The hospital setting in an emergency situation is a difficult dynamic to assess. In all other societal settings we are allowed to meet people, size them up, and figure out if we can trust them or not. When meeting a doctor, nurse or staff member in a hospital hallway, there is no time for pleasantries or evaluations of character. In spite of that, I wanted to grab everyone that walked by and explain to them who it was they were trying to save. I wanted to shout about Jeff's life and explain just why we needed them all to be as diligent and intelligent as they'd ever been in their lives.

This is our brother! Our best friend! He's a great husband, father, son and nephew! He's an executive chef who makes the best stuffed peppers in the world! He has the world's greatest sense of humor, and we can't make it without him So save him right now, damn it!

Of course, I didn't actually say that, but the words were racing through my mind at break-neck speed like a whirling blur of emotions that I just couldn't grasp. Despite the frenzy in my head, the action all around me seemed to be moving too slowly. By the time I checked my telephone messages, my father had joined me in the emergency room area. The sight of my father, a beacon of strength in all of the years I was growing up, was absolutely stunning. There was a vacant, lost look on his face.

I had never seen such a look in my father's eyes, and he glanced at me, and then looked behind the curtain at Jeff, who was slowly slipping into unconsciousness.

"What happened?" he asked, but Dad wasn't looking for an answer. Instead, his face contorted in pure anguish, and the reality of where we were standing crashed down on my shoulders once more.

"He'll be fine," I whispered, but Dad's face told me otherwise. It was all either of us could do to not crumple to the floor right then and there.

"It'll be okay," Dad whispered back. "We've never done anything to anyone. God will take care of Jeff." Yet our shared tears brought a lifetime of fears to that shitty little examining room.

I headed down the hall in an effort to get a handle on the dim terror that was swimming around in my brain, but all I could think of was the last long telephone conversation that I'd had with Jeff.

On January 25, on my way home from a book event in Providence Rhode Island, my cell phone rang as Jeff made his usual morning call.

"How'd the event go?" he asked.

"I got an award for Nobody's Home," I said.

"That's awesome," he said. "It was a good book."

"Now I'm stuck in the Baltimore airport and the plane is delayed again."

"Ah, that's too bad," Jeff said. "We're going to head down to the YMCA. I'm bringing the family. I thought maybe you'd bring the boys and we could get a game of hoops going."

I wished I could be there, of course. I was sick of the travel, tired of working my way through security and agitated that I was still on the road halfway through my Sunday afternoon. "Give Kathy a call," I said. "Maybe she'll bring the boys down."

"If not, I'll run a mile or so. I tried to do it the other day and I almost collapsed. It's horrible how out of shape I am."

"Yeah, what about me?" I asked.

We both laughed. "Speaking of dead animals, I ordered the side of beef," he said. "It'll be ready the first week in April. That should give you enough time to come up with an excuse as to why you can't help pick it up."

"I'll be there," I said.

Jeff didn't answer right away.

"By the way, I finished reading Blind Spot last night," he said finally. "It was awesome, but I have a little advice for you."

"What's that?" I was fully expecting a wise-ass comment about how I had stolen his ideas, or how the book was successful because he had inspired me somehow.

"You need to enjoy life instead of trying to understand it," he said.

"What're you? Plato?" I asked as I laughed it off.

"I'm just saying. Life doesn't have to be a hassle. You can have some fun."

For one reason or another, the idea that I should be having fun with life kept gnawing at my brain. How would life ever be fun again if Jeff were too sick to enjoy it with me? Thankfully, I didn't have to wander the halls of Mercy Hospital for too long before the other members of the family joined Dad, Lynn and me.   But the fear in everyone's eyes reflected the grim fact that this was not the usual family gathering.

My parents, John and Lynda, spent every moment of their lives trying to build the family that was slowly gathering in the cloud of fear in the halls of Mercy Hospital. There were six children altogether, Corinne, John, myself, Jim, Jeff and Carrie Lynn. We grew together as best friends and loyal buddies, but as we came together on that bitterly cold afternoon, we all seemed to understand that we'd need every ounce of our love for one another.

Before long, John's wife Dana, Jim's wife Lisa and Corinne's husband Chuck all arrived on the scene, looking for answers. Carrie, who lived near Baltimore, was literally taking the first plane to Buffalo. Lynn was in the unenviable position of having to speak with the doctors to see what the plan of attack was. Lynn emerged from the examining room into the hallway. Her eyes, which were normally dancing with the excitement of seeing all of us together, were distant and vague. My poor sister-in-law looked as though she might pass out right there onto the cold tile floor. "They're going to do an angiogram and then they may have to operate to relieve some of the pressure on the brain. It's really serious."

Once more I had the extreme misfortune of turning to face my father. Tears were streaming down his face, and I considered all that he might be thinking. After years of working so hard to raise us and protect us from harm, Dad must have felt absolutely useless as he considered that Jeff were about to undergo brain surgery. Being a parent of three children myself and having had to face a life-threatening tumor in one of my own boys provided me with a bit of insight, but I had no idea how I could possibly be strong for my father when my own heart was threatening to explode.

"Is it a stroke? An aneurysm? I mean, what is a brain bleed?" I asked.

The questions were coming from all angles. What in the hell had happened?

In 2003, Jeff had landed a job as an executive chef at the Gow School in South Wales, New York, just a twenty-minute drive from his home. It was Jeff's dream job for a number of reasons, including working with a close-knit faculty and staff who'd grown to be special friends. Standing in the hallway outside the emergency room doors, I turned to face one of Jeff's closest friends at the school, Paul Rose. I shook Paul's hand. His face was a mask of desperation and despair.

"What the hell happened?" I asked.

"He ate his lunch, and his face was red because he'd eaten a really hot pepper. He headed back into his office, but then stepped back out, asked the secretary to call 911 and went back in and sat down. I recognized the signs of a stroke or a brain injury and we got the ambulance to him in a hurry. They were there within seven minutes."

A wave of gratitude swept through me as I realized that Paul's quick thinking would ultimately save Jeff's life. What kind of trouble would he be in if he hadn't been transported to the hospital in a hurry?

Thinking back on my own son's medical emergency, I chased the negative thoughts far away. Negative thoughts are the devil speaking, I thought. We don't have any room for him here today.

My brother-in-law Chuck greeted me in the hallway near the hospital emergency room just after I concluded my little pep talk to myself.

"He's going to be okay," Chuck said.

I considered my brother-in-law and how he'd been accepted into the family. I thought of all that Chuck meant to Jeff, and vice versa, and I knew that the outcome of the story was going to have a profound affect on so, so many people.

"He has to be okay," I said, and for the first time since the news broke, I couldn't chase away the sob that had been building inside of me. Chuck pulled me into a heavy embrace, and we cried together.

As a unit, the extended Fazzolari family had always been extremely proficient at getting things done. In one way or another, we were all successful in our work and in our home lives. We were facing a crisis, but individually we were all equipped to deal with the emergency. As we gathered in the hallway outside of the Intensive Care Unit, our words of fear were replaced by the strong convictions of our hearts.

"Jeff's a strong kid," Jim said. "All those years of working construction and battling his back pain. Man, I'm telling you, he's stronger than the rest of us."

"He's the strongest son I have," my father agreed. "He's going to be okay."

Yet there was still no way of knowing for sure, and the shadow of doubt that was creeping through my quickly fading optimism scared me more than anything else in my life, including my son Jake's life-saving operation. It had been Jeff who'd been beside me during those anxious moments back in 2001. I left the family for a moment, retreating to the men's room where I splashed water on my face and recounted the days leading up to Jake's surgery.

Four-year-old Jacob had awoken on a Sunday morning, struggling to breath. He was rushed to the hospital where a huge tumor was discovered, and for the next six weeks, he fought to stay alive.

The devastation of hearing this news was almost too much for me to bear. One of the very first telephone calls I made was to Jeff, who, through the years, was my sounding board of logic. He listened patiently to me as I wailed into the phone, and then he stopped me with a few simple sentences.

"It's all about faith," he said. "You have the faith. Just make sure everyone around you sees it, including Jake. Get tough with this and be determined. He'll be fine."

During Jake's treatment, the Yankees were in the World Series for the fourth consecutive year after spoiling us rotten with three straight championships. Game 1 was scheduled for a Saturday night, just a week before Jake's operation to remove the tumor. Jeff called our house just an hour before the game was to start. "Come on over and watch the Yankees," he said.

"I don't feel like going to a party," I answered.

"It isn't a party. It's just me and you," he said. "It'll be good for you."

I was certainly hesitant, but I made the short trip to Jeff's home, and we sat together and watched Arizona soundly trash the Yankees in Game 1. Of course, the game was secondary to the time that we shared. We sipped a couple of Heinekens and I wondered aloud about the choice of beer.

"When I heard Jake was sick, something clicked," Jeff said. "I decided that from here on out I'm going with the good stuff. Life can be miserable. Why waste time drinking the cheap stuff?"

Despite the lopsided score of the game, Jeff and I were tuned in until the very last out was recorded. As I was leaving his basement, he repeated his testament to faith.

"Do you really think it's all up to God?" I asked him. "I mean, I know what we've learned, but the doubt creeps in."

"It all boils down to the things you can't hold," he said. "If it isn't about love and faith and hope, what is it about? I thought that Springsteen and the nuns taught you better than that."

On a night when I was shaken to the very core, he had made me laugh.

"It'll be fine, you'll see," he said. "The Yankees will come back to win and Jake will be fine."

As it turned out, Jeff was right about just one of the two things. The Yankees did not win.

The entire family was in the waiting room as Jake's surgeon relayed the good news: "The surgery was successful. Jake will be okay."

Jeff, front and center, gripped me in a crushing bear hug. "See, stupid, it's all about faith," he said as tears glistened his eyes.

And it was all about faith now. We would need to rely on faith, family and friends, and before too long, it was apparent that we'd have ample amounts of each. Within just a couple of hours the hallway outside the Intensive Care Unit was filled with people. Jeff's good friends, Mike Livecchi, Jeff Popple, Chris Miller, Jeff Renaldo and Chris Heinold immediately joined our family to figure it all out. There were hugs all around, but there was precious little information to share. Someone mentioned that the first twenty-four to seventy-two hours after such an event was the crucial time, but in my mind, I wasn't exactly sure what we were dealing with. The first three days of treatment were crucial to what? Jeff wasn't going to die, was he?

Mike scrolled through information on his Blackberry about the type of stroke that we imagined it to be. There were plenty of pages of text, but I remembered from Jake's surgery that it was easy to get bogged down in information overload. Still, as Mike waded through the data, we all stood by him and waited for him to exclaim that it would be okay, and that this was just one of Jeff's elaborate practical jokes. We were praying that he was ready to trick us again and that he'd be leaping from the bed, screaming, "Surprise!"

In those first few hours, Lynn was in an awful position, a position that no young mother of three should ever be in. Although she was receiving a lion's share of the hugs, there wasn't much that could be said that could possibly take away her fear or anxiety. Still, she stood tall and after returning from a consultation with one of the doctors, delivered the first bit of news.

"They're going to work on alleviating some of the pressure on his brain by getting rid the blood. Then they'll be able to see what they're up against. They plan on doing that at seven p.m."

I turned away from the scene for a brief second to gather my own thoughts. One thing at a time, I lectured myself. It'll be a process, maybe a long process, but he'll be okay.

I was just concluding my internal conversation when Chuck relayed the only other useful piece of information to come out of those first few hours.

"Carrie's flight is coming in by six," he said. "We'll pick her up at the airport, and she should be here by the time they perform the operation."

"That's good," I said. "We all belong here."

I spun on my heel, turning away from Chuck so that he wouldn't see me cry. Unfortunately for me, as I turned I saw the tortured face of my anguished mother. How could I possibly help her? How could any of us help each other? We were all too heartbroken.

It was a day that held so much promise. I thought of the Springsteen album and how excited Jeff and I had been.

Fucking Bruce! I thought.

I chased the thought away by hugging my crying mother.

Chapter II – Life Itself

January 27, 2009 Don't ask yourself what the world needs. Ask what makes you come alive, and go do it. Because what the world needs is people who have come alive. Howard Thurman

Just before the operation was to begin, two of the doctors walked past John, Jim, my father and me in the hallway. "He's as strong as an ox," John said to them. John's eyes were full of tears, but his voice was strong and reflected the determination in all of our hearts.

"He's going to have to be," the doctor said. "He's got a lot of work ahead of him."

"He'll be playing basketball in no time," John said as his voice cracked with emotion.

"That'd be a miracle," the doctor said as he disappeared behind the operating room door.

As the Mercy Hospital staff of doctors and nurses performed the procedure on Jeff, family and friends gathered in the surgical waiting room. There were plenty of tears, hugs and anxious moments, but determination and faith were also making an appearance. We were a strong family, and we were sure that love would get us through this. Our love was something that we'd relied on all of our lives, and it would not fail us now.

The saying in North Collins, a small town located about twenty miles south of Buffalo, had always been that if you'd seen one Fuzzy you'd seen them all. We Fazzolari siblings, affectionately known as "the Fuzzys'", had always been each other's best friends in the world. From Corinne on down to Carrie Lynn, with four boys in the middle, we were as close as a family could be. There wasn't a single day that passed, as adults, when we did not speak together. There were hardly ever any cross words between us, and our love was absolutely undeniable. It was a love that we'd learned at the hands of John and Lynda, and we would certainly carry it through all our lives. We would need every second of that love to get through this ordeal.

During Jeff's procedure, Carrie and Corinne took control of the situation, gathering all twenty of us in a circle of prayer in the waiting room.

Midway through the prayer, I felt dizzy, as though I were about to pass out. I reached up to wipe away what I thought were just remnants of tears clinging to my nose. But when I glanced down at my right hand I saw a splatter of blood between my thumb and forefinger. Soon, the blood covered the front of my shirt as my wife Kathy and Corinne hustled to find tissues. I tried to stop the flow of blood by tipping my head back and pinching the base of my nose. It was the first time in my life that I'd ever had a nosebleed!

Chuck guided me down the hall, into the elevator and out the front doors of the hospital. The cold evening air smacked us in the face as the automatic doors closed behind us.

"What the fuck is going on?" I screamed to Chuck.

"We all have to calm down," Chuck said. "It's stress, worry and pain. We have to group together here. We'll get on top of it. We have a strong family. We have a lot of faith."

Chuck's arm was around my shoulder. The nosebleed was under control. The cold air hurt my lungs when I finally took a deep breath. In that moment I considered another place and time when life had showed its ugly side.

I can recall exactly where I was on the moment when it

felt that my childhood officially ended. I was seated in my home office, working on a report, contemplating dinner and the kids' return from school. There was just so much to do and so little time to get it all done. The ringing cell phone yanked me out of the frenzy building in my head. Yet it was a friendly call. My brother-in-law Chuck was on the line.

"What's up?" I said. I was always ready to hear from Chuck. The family consensus was that Chuck was a perfect fit and a wonderful husband to our older sister, Corinne.

"Bad news," Chuck said simply. "Your sister has breast cancer."

"Dude, it's April Fool's Day," I said.

"I wish I were joking," Chuck answered.

I felt a rush of pure fear race through my body. Goose-flesh ran down both my arms. "It's for sure?" I asked. "Was it a lump? Do they know what they're going to do? Did they catch it early?"

Chuck wasn't ready for the onslaught of questions, but he had a favor to ask. "Can you contact some of the people you know at Women & Children's Hospital and see what they know about Corinne's doctors? They're talking about operating sometime next week."

The rush of fear was not even close to subsiding. How could any of this be true? Would she be all right? A family friend, Kathy George, had recently lost her battle with breast cancer. "I'll contact Children's," I said.

"I just spoke to Jeff and Carrie. I have a few more calls to make," Chuck said.

"Well, hang in there," I said lamely.

"We'll get through this," Chuck said, but in his voice I heard the same fear that was boiling in my veins.

I closed my cell phone and stared at the half-finished report on my computer desktop. Finishing writing the report could certainly wait. I grabbed the phone again and looked through my list of contacts. The sound of my ring tone nearly caused me to jump out of my skin. It was Jeff on the other end of the line.

"Did you hear?" he asked.

"Yeah, Chuck just called me," I said.

"It sucks," Jeff said. "I'm having a tough time understanding that life can just turn on a dime like that. I was just thinking about how things were starting to calm down a little. I was in a real good mood, and now this."

"Yeah, she'll be okay," I said.

I wasn't sure if I believed what I was saying, but I thought of Jeff and how busy his life had become. I heard the hurt in his voice, and having been through Jake's operation and recovery, I felt as if I had to be the calm, reassuring voice.

"You know, God is on our side," Jeff said, "but bad things happen to everyone. One of these times it isn't going to work out for us like we want it to."

"Jeff, that's just negative thinking. We need to stay positive."

"I know, but you know what I mean?"

"She'll be fine."

"I just can't imagine," Jeff said. "I'm just so sorry that she has to go through any of this."

"We all are," I responded.

"I've always wondered when life was going to reach out and grab us," Jeff said.

"She'll be okay. You said it yourself, we have God on our side."

Jeff paused for a long moment. I wondered if he'd just hung up as he normally did when he was tired of talking. "I'm thinking of the Bruce song, Devils & Dust," he said. "The line where he says, 'Sometimes faith just ain't enough.'"

"Dude, it's going to be fine."

I'm not sure how our conversation ended on that day, but a week later, we were all gathered in the waiting room at the Women & Children's Hospital of Buffalo as Corinne went through an operation that we prayed would set her on the road to recovery.

A surgical waiting room is a scary place to be yet during Jake's operation Corinne had led us in whiling the time away. She had brought enough food to feed the entire hospital, and her good humor had carried the day. During her operation, it was Jeff's turn to take charge. He brought food and walked from person to person, bringing smiles to the worried faces of everyone gathered. The minutes passed like hours, but soon enough the doctor returned to the room with the news that we desperately needed.

"Things went well. You can see her in a little while."

I recall hugging everyone in the room, including Jeff, who tried desperately to hide the tears that had gathered in the corners of his eyes.

"I told you she'd be all right," he cried. "I told you faith would be rewarded."

A few hours later, I was seated beside John, Carrie and Jeff. We had just ordered a beer at a bar close to the hospital.

"This is as bad as life can get," Jeff said as he raised his beer.

"This has been a good day," I said.

"I know," Jeff said, "but I can't stop thinking that the price you pay for love is fear. I hate being afraid that something bad is going to happen to someone I love."

Amen to that, my brother. Amen.

Back outside of Mercy Hospital, my thoughts shifted from Corinne's battle to what we were facing that night. What if this time faith isn't enough? I thought.

"Positive thoughts," Chuck said, as though he were reading my mind. "We need to stay strong for everyone."

My dear brother-in-law was right on the mark. We would dig deep, and we would endure.

"Think of Jeff being here if this were happening to someone else," Chuck said. "He'd hold us all together. He'd be painting our faces with nail polish as we sat in the wheelchair."

"I know," I said and I choked out a laugh that mixed with tears and dried blood.

"We need to be strong," Chuck whispered. "Strong."

Chuck and I re-entered the hospital and headed back to the family. Two of the strongest men that I'd ever met were waiting for us back in the surgical waiting room. John and Jim stood side by side, chatting quietly about what needed to be done. I was certain that Jeff's big brother and little brother had come to a consensus on it all, and despite their worry, they were sure that it would all work out.

"He'll get through it," John whispered, and he hugged me. "What're you bleeding about, you big baby?"

I shrugged. I'd always looked up to John. He was just eleven months older than I was. We had grown up together, playing, fighting and laughing all the way.

Jim's hand found my other shoulder. Jim was closer in age to Jeff and had chosen his little brother as best man for his wedding. Jim was one tough guy whose heart was as big as his head.

"He's got too much going for him to let this stop him," Jim said.

"I know, I know," I said.

"We have to keep an eye on Mom and Dad," Jim said.

The message was getting through to me. I was going to have to try to be strong, as strong as my brothers always seemed to be. I took a deep breath, and we waited.

I absolutely hated being in that waiting room, with the squawk of the overhead speakers calling for doctors and the lights and sounds of the hospital. The white walls, the hand sanitizer around every corner, the hustling nurses and the smells of sickness were making me sick. I didn't want to be in the hospital for any reason.

The wait wasn't too long this time. Soon, the doctor joined us in the room to relay news of the procedure. "It went well," he said. "We can move forward from here. We took care of some of the pressure. Jeff will be sedated in an effort to locate the source of the bleed so we can get control of the situation. Time will be the healer."

In a matter of hours, Jeff was settled into ICU room four. He was sedated and intubated, and the staff explained that he would most likely be out for the night. My family migrated back to the waiting room on the fourth floor. For the first time in a while I found myself standing beside Kathy. We were going to have to make arrangements to get back to our lives in some fashion, and I knew this was on Kathy's mind. The boys had been home alone, with Matthew serving as the boss, since the early afternoon.

"What're we going to do?" Kathy asked.

In a split second I considered how much she loved Jeff and what his situation was doing to her. I also considered how much I loved her and how I was going to need her strength in the coming months. "I'm not leaving," I said.

"I didn't imagine you would," she said, "but where are you going to sleep?"

The waiting room was a picture of absolute discomfort. There was a small television and about seven hard plastic chairs lined up in the dimly lit room. A tall, humming Pepsi machine provided the only comfort whatsoever.

"I won't sleep," I said. "Maybe by his bedside. We need to get Mom and Dad home, and Lynn too. God, someone has to stay with the kids."

Yet before I was even able to throw my two cents in and tell the others, everything had been settled. Just as we had done in all of our years together, we slipped comfortably into our roles. There was little doubt that we'd work together to get through the pain. Corinne was the levelheaded leader, and with Chuck's help, all of our roles were clearly defined. Carrie and I would spend the night, taking turns to check on Jeff every so often. Mom and Dad would head home for the best possible rest that they could get, and Lynn would do the same, picking up the kids along the way and trying her best to be strong for them.

Hours later, Carrie and I shared our eleventh cup of coffee in the now deserted hallway just off the Intensive Care Unit. The hallway lights were bright, but there was much less activity on the floor. Occasionally a door would open and close as a nurse, doctor, or resident moved through, but for the most part, it was just Carrie and I sitting in the hallway. Jeff was heavily sedated, but we were so far from sleep that we were laughing at anything and everything. Stories of Jeff drifted into our minds, and we shared a lot in those couple of hours.

Carrie grabbed her I-pod. "The Bruce album is awesome," she said.

"It really is," I answered, "but it's hard to listen to. I want to talk to Jeff about it."

"You will," Carrie said. "Time is the healer. We can put in the time as long as he's going to be all right."

"I know," I said. "I'll sit here until about 2012 if I have to."

Carrie put the I-pod ear bud into position and began singing along with the song Working on a Dream. "I'm going to try to sleep," she said.

"Me too," I answered. "I'm going to check on Jeff once

more, and then I'll lie on the floor in there."

I headed down the hall toward room four. I instinctively took a glob of hand sanitizer from a nearby wall dispenser and edged up slowly to the bedside. The lights were off in the ICU, but nurses were moving back and forth, doing their job in the quiet of the middle of the night.

When my eyes adjusted to the dark and I got a good look at Jeff under the covers, I shuddered in fear. He looked drawn, out of it and just plain sick. His eyes were pressed closed, and tears were escaping and rolling down his cheeks. I wondered if he knew how scared we all were. I wondered if he even understood what was happening. I've loved him every second that he's been on this planet, I thought. God, please heal him.

The monitors were flashing numbers that meant little to me. The tube down his throat and his closed eyes were almost too much for me to bear.

"Rest, my brother," I whispered. "It's going to be okay."

I shuffled back down the hall. Carrie was on the floor, asleep, the I-pod still anchored firmly in her ears. I stepped over her and headed to an empty piece of carpet. I pretty much fell onto my back, saying the words of the Our Father as I settled in. A clear, distinct memory of Jeff rattled through my weary brain.

In 1972, at seven years old, I had come to understand my rank in the family as the little brother to Corinne and John and the older brother to Jim, Jeff and Carrie. I also began to understand that we were all united and that together we could make or break the family dynamic. When we all ganged up, Mom and Dad didn't have a chance, but Dad definitely had a loud, booming voice that kept us on the straight and narrow. We clearly understood that there was an all-for-one and one-for-all element to our day-by-day living.

Early one morning, I heard noises coming from the

kitchen. I checked the small alarm clock in the bedroom I shared with my brother, John. He was still asleep, with good reason; it was just a little after six a.m. on a Saturday. I knew that whoever was up and making the racket in the kitchen was on the verge of getting into some real trouble.

I stepped into the kitchen to see a mound of flour, sugar, brown sugar and coffee in the center of the room. In the middle of the pile was a glass pitcher that had been shattered. Sitting off to the left of the pile was two-year-old Jeff. He had a measuring cup in his left hand and he smiled at me broadly.

"What're you doing?" I asked. "Mom and Dad are going to go crazy!"

"I'm making Kool-Aid," Jeff said proudly, "Want some?"

I didn't want anything to do with his little recipe for disaster. He was just coming off a punishment for sharing a stick of pepperoni with our dog, Ricky.

"You're in a lot of trouble," I said.

"Just making Kool-Aid," he answered.

I slipped off to sleep with the memory on my brain, but I woke quickly, alertly as if I were being physically threatened. I struggled off the floor and back out into the hallway. Less than two minutes later, Carrie's eyes were wide open.

"How long did we sleep?" she asked.

I glanced at the numbers on my cell phone. "I slept for eleven minutes!" I said, laughing.

"That must mean I got about thirteen," Carrie replied with a giggle. "What do you say we grab a coffee?"

"Right after you check on Jeff," I said.

Carrie stretched as though she'd slept for ten hours. She groaned loudly as she raised both arms high above her head. I considered how she had grown with Jeff, just sharing so much. As children they'd painted each other with nail polish and cut each other's hair. As adults, they shared the joys of marriage, children and laughter. I considered Jeff to be my best friend, but it suddenly dawned on me that Corinne, John, Jim and Carrie most likely did, too.

"What's your favorite song on the CD?" she asked.

"Life Itself, I guess," I said. "Life Itself."

Chapter III – Kingdom of Days

January 29, 2009   Childhood is not from birth to a certain age and at a certain age the child is grown, and puts away childish things. Childhood is the kingdom where nobody dies.   Edna St. Vincent Millay.

In the early afternoon hours, two days after Jeff suffered the stroke, I turned over in the bed after a short, fitful nap. The shock of what was happening swept over me like a wave, and I tried hard to slip back into some sort of sleep that would allow me to spend another night on the hospital waiting room floor, but my mind would have none of it.

"This is Jeff we're talking about," I whispered to the quiet room. "God, are you listening? He has a wife and three kids depending on him. He's a good man. Come on, please!"

I struggled to the shower, glancing in the bathroom mirror as I passed. The bags were heavy under my eyes, but that didn't concern me much. I had a fleeting thought of work, and decided that I would have to make a couple of calls. My boss and good friend, Robert Rayo, had called in the middle of yesterday's chaos to let me know that the company had my back.

"Do what you need to do," Rob said. "Your family comes first."

As the warm water hit me, my mind played a quick trick on me, taking me back in time to a day just after Jeff's wedding. We'd shared so many days that it was almost impossible to gauge what specific memories might come rushing back to me as he recovered.

Lynn and Jeff began their married life together in an

apartment in Hamburg, NY. As was the custom, friends and family helped orchestrate the move into the new home, and as we carried the possessions into the apartment, we were all struck by the idea that the young marriage was absolutely perfect in every way. The morning of the move, however, Jeff appeared extremely tired.

Jeff had accepted a position as an executive chef at Buffalo State College. He was responsible for the supervision and management of all operations, including the preparation of all foods and design of ice carvings for various functions. He was disciplining the work staff, ordering the foods and handling cost analysis for the operation.

"You know what blows my mind?" he asked as we maneuvered a couch through the front door of his new apartment. Jeff was wearing a Yankee shirt with a photo of Derek Jeter on the front. A chain around his neck held a small gold Italian horn.

"What's that?"

"It's that a lot of people don't have much of a work ethic. Man, I'll tell you, the long hours are taking a real toll on my back, but some of the people working for me just don't get it. They think they should be the boss as soon as you hire them, and they don't feel as if they have to work for anything."

"Yeah, it's frustrating," I said.

We placed the big green couch in a corner of the apartment and adjusted it to look just right.

"I mean, I'd love to have a brand new house right now so that we can start a family, but there are dues to pay."

"You'll get there," I said.

We headed back down the stairs to grab another piece of furniture.

"All I want to do with my life is build a family," he said. "I want to give our kids the chances that Mom and Dad gave us."

I was nearing the bottom of the stairs, thinking that I was extremely proud of my younger brother. He certainly understood all that truly mattered. Despite all the comic relief he had offered to everyone in the family, he was certainly, ethically, on the right track.

"You might make it after all," I said.

The moment I completed that sentence was the exact moment that Jeff chose to kick my right leg, which made contact with my left leg and forced me to tumble down the last three steps as Jeff hooted and hollered behind me.

I lay flat out on the floor at the landing as he stood over the top of me and gave an emphatic safe signal.

Just perfect.

As I dressed, I called Corinne at the hospital. She was spending time at Jeff's bedside with Lynn, Carrie, John, Jim and Chuck.

"He's still sedated," Corinne reported, "but no news is good news, right? Take the time you need. We have to work together on this. There have been plenty of visitors. We need you for the night shift."

It sounded as though my big sister was in at least a bit of control. I understood that we were all torn apart, but moment after precious moment was all that mattered. Everything else could wait.

I grabbed a quick sandwich and headed for the front door. There in the hallway was the air mattress that my wife had packed for my trip back to the ICU. What would I do without her?

I drove to the hospital in silence. I still couldn't bring myself to listen to the Springsteen album. The fleeting thought that ran through my mind was that I wouldn't listen to it until Jeff could hear it, too. However, there was one single word that I couldn't avoid.

"Why?" I yelled to the interior of my truck. "Why is this

happening?" I scanned the grey skies for a hint of an answer. The clouds hung so low that it seemed as if they were pushing straight down onto my head. "Why God, or whatever the hell is up there? Why?"

Jeff had been in good shape. He never had high blood pressure or other physical problems that would lead to this mess. His back had caused him pain for years, but a bad back didn't cause a stroke, did it? Could it have been the pain medications? Was it all due to stress or long work hours?

Hell, he'd eaten a big lunch and spoke normally with me twenty minutes before it happened. Why was he fighting for his life now?

I arrived at the hospital expecting to see at least one of my siblings, but my first step off the elevator told me that there would be plenty of comforting arms to step into should the need arise. Corinne, Chuck, Carrie, John, Jim, Mom, Dad, Lynn and Paul Rose from the Gow School were all gathered in the cramped little waiting room. There were a few bags of snacks gathered on the small table beside the hard brown chair.

"He's doing okay," Jim said to me as I tossed the gym bag with a few essentials into the space beside the groaning Pepsi machine. "They are concerned that he might have some paralysis on his left side, but it's too soon to tell. He's stable."

I made my way to Corinne. I was sure that my big sister was holding it together for everyone. She was scribbling a note into a green marble-printed notebook.

"I figured we could share things by writing in the notebook," she said. "That way we won't forget anything, and we can go back and forth, to encourage each other."

"It's a great idea," I said. "How's Lynn doing? I didn't get a chance to talk to her."

"She's in the room with Jeff. She's hanging in there,"

Corinne said, "but if this takes a while, we're all going to have to pitch in to give her some rest."

"We'll handle it," I said. "We'll figure out a schedule or something. He's going to be as good as new in a couple of days anyway."

Corinne glanced down at the notebook. Her big brown eyes told me that she needed me to be right in my assessment.

I eased into the chair beside my brother John. He was working a word search puzzle, but the worry lines on his face told me that he was less concerned about finding the next word than he was about his brother. John had been the first one in the family to get married. Growing up, we'd all been so close that the idea that one of us would be moving out to start his or her own family was sort of scary. Watching John work that puzzle, I reflected back on the days of John's wedding.

Of course, as life moved forward there were changes all around. One of the most significant changes in our lives came in the form of a pretty young girl named Dana Colantino. For reasons unknown to John's siblings, Dana fell in love with John, and before too long the two were inseparable. The courtship seemed to go by in a flash, and before you knew it, we were at the rehearsal dinner for the wedding.

What immediately comes to mind about the wedding of John and Dana wasn't the beautiful moment in the church, it wasn't the unbelievable party that followed the nuptials, it wasn't even how beautiful the couple looked as they left the hall as man and wife. For John and his three brothers, it was all about the night before.

We returned from the rehearsal dinner with our minds on a few beers. Thankfully, our parents had a foosball table and a billiard table in the basement. Springsteen's Darkness on the Edge of Town was John's favorite album, and we started the four-man party believing that a few beers would allow John to unwind before his big day.

The foosball match-up was John and Jeff against Jim and me, and it lasted for hours. It was my responsibility to keep Jeff from scoring, but his lightning quick hands caused me fits for most of the evening.

Yet there was something almost subdued about the evening, as if each song that ended and each goal collected was bringing us that much closer to the conclusion of our days together. John would be out of the house, a married man. The four of us weren't sure what that was going to do to our friendship. There was no doubting that Dana would fit perfectly into our lives, but we were blood brothers, and it certainly felt as if something were ending.

Despite knowing that the next day would be a long, wonderful event, we continued on into the night with our party. The foosball match turned into a game of eight ball. Darkness on the Edge of Town gave way to Born in the USA and still we played on. It all got a little hairy when Jeff said, "Let's play pool hockey."

"What's that?" John asked.

"We stand on opposite ends of the table. We each get three balls and we get to fire them in the direction of the other guy's pocket. If it goes in you get a goal."

"How do we defend the pocket?" I asked.

"With your hands," Jeff said. "And if the ball leaves the table, you fight for it."

I cast a doubting eye on Jim and John. To me, the game sounded like pure lunacy.

"I'm in," Jim said.

"Me too," John added.

For the next two hours, we rifled billiard balls at one another's hands as we tried to defend the goal. The balls were bouncing all over the basement too, and the game soon turned to pure football. I had swollen hands, a bloody nose and sore kidneys from where Jeff punched me after jumping on me as I slid on the floor chasing one loose ball.

The classic ending of the evening came at just a little before two in the morning. John threw a ball that glanced off my hand and clipped me on the shoulder. The ball went sailing into the storage closet just behind the pool table. I rushed into the closet, believing that there wasn't anything in the world that could stop me from retrieving the ball and depositing it in the goal. I never made it to the ball. Jeff's diving tackle knocked me off my feet, and John and Jim piled on top.

Just hours before the first family wedding, we were in a pile on the floor of the storage closet. We were laughing, punching and sharing. That night we felt as if our closeness as brothers was coming to an end, but we were wrong. It was all just beginning.

The wedding reception was held at the Knights of Columbus in Hamburg. For the very first time the family gathered in celebration of adding a new member. Jeff was unbelievably caught up in the pomp and circumstance, and he held court on the dance floor and in the area directly behind the bar.

The end of the evening came with an invitation to say a few words to the new bride and groom, and Jeff gladly grabbed the microphone as the videotape ran. A cummerbund wrapped tightly around his head, Jeff looked directly into the camera. Standing alone, with the alcohol hampering his ability to put a great thought together, he hesitated a moment before uttering the one sentence that is forever linked to the marriage of John and Dana.

"To John and Dana, we both love you all."
***

Back in the hospital waiting room I could feel my father's eyes upon me. "You watch, he'll be as good as new," dad said.

The words brought me out of the memory trance, and I stood up and regained my wits. "I know," I said. "We just got to do what we can do to help each other through. Is Mom doing okay?"

"She didn't sleep much. Neither of us slept more than an hour at a time."

I stole a peek at my sleep spot from the night before. The hard floor wasn't very inviting, but at least the air mattress would soften my vigil tonight. "We just have to suck it up for awhile," I said. "I can remember when Jake was sick, the doctors explained that we were no good without proper rest. You don't need to get sick on top of this."

My father wasn't much interested in my lecture. Instead, he pulled me close to him and gave me a forceful hug, "I love you," he said.

"Me too," I managed to reply, but the swell of emotion took me away from the room and down the hall. "I'm going to check on him."

It's virtually impossible to walk the halls of a hospital, particularly in a critical care unit, and not feel the pain. Normal life consists of not really considering the end of life much, perhaps even fearing the inevitable conclusion we all must face, but the possibility of the end is echoed off the four walls of the critical care unit. As I walked along, I tried desperately to push it far from my mind. I ignored the smell of what? Sickness? I tried not to think of the pure white walls or consider those who were running from room to room, offering care to the sick. Instead, I considered the life that had been gathering all around us.

The flow of visitors to Jeff's bedside had been constant since that very first moment. Uncle Jim, his face a mask of desperation, had stopped by with our cousins Jamie and Kristan. Like everyone else, they were confused as to why Jeff was in such a predicament, and the comfort that they offered was twisted up in the confusion of their own grief. Yet they were not alone. Cousins Tony and Wendy Fazzolari had made the hour drive from Gasport, while cousins Carol, Chris and Mike Wittmeyer had delivered gifts and well wishes from Olean. The stream of well-wishers continued throughout the day and into the evening.

As I approached room four that afternoon, I was distracted for a moment by a man in a wheelchair in the center of the hall. My first thought was that the man had to be at least ninety-years old. He was howling in pain, and the front of his loose hanging hospital gown was covered with a dried yellow substance. I wasn't sure what I should do as I passed by, but the best plan of action seemed to be to duck my head and struggle by. I got a good, close-up whiff of what I'd been smelling and nearly gagged as I passed.

"Why don't they just let me die?" the man screamed.

His shriek produced the attention that he needed as a nurse hurried to him, passing just an inch from my shoulder, as I ducked into the room that held my brother.

In seeing Jeff, the reality of the situation struck me straight in the solar plexus once more. Why did that old man get to live to ninety while Jeff was struggling after a mere thirty-eight years into this bullshit life? We'd done a lot of praying in the halls of the hospital, but what the hell were we praying to? There were babies who were dying moments after they took their first breath of air, and there was just so much despair. God? Are you kidding me? How could there possibly be a God?

I struggled for a breath as I gazed at my brother. Tubes lay everywhere, and it occurred to me that if he were aware of all that was going on, he'd be really pissed off that he wasn't able to entertain all of his visitors. If he'd known that the list of visitors to his bedside included most of his friends, co-workers and family, he'd have been concerned about their entertainment and, of course, the menu.

"Hang in there, kid," I whispered. "You need a lot of rest today. Every hour that passes is important."

There were a few gifts on the desk near the window, including a football that was still in the box and a copy of the new Rolling Stone magazine with Springsteen's photo on the front cover. I'd read the article a couple of days before, and I hadn't yet had the chance to discuss it with Jeff.

"That's what I miss most of all," I whispered. "I miss talking to you so much."

I touched my brother on the left arm and told him to rest well. I left the room and sidled past the still-scream-ing old man.

God? Are you kidding me? What God?

Within ten feet of each other was a young man with so much to live for and an old man shouting down the halls for the chance to finally leave. Even God would have to admit it was a ridiculous notion.

Back in the waiting room, the visitors for the day had cleared out, leaving me alone with the sound of that fuck-ing groaning, whirring, Pepsi machine and with my sister Corinne. I kicked at the machine as I plopped down in one of the hard plastic chairs.

"Do you realize that that machine makes noise all night long?" I said.

"It doesn't work, either," Corinne said. "I've watched seven people lose their money in it. I try to tell them but the stupid bastards stick their dollars in anyway."

I laughed. "People need to see things for themselves," I said. "They think they'll be the one to make it work."

Corinne handed me a cup of coffee and the green

notebook that held the information of the day.

"There's some funny crap in there," Corinne said. "We've been trying to blow off steam by making each other laugh."

"The family trait," I said.

As I sipped the coffee, I scanned the names of some of the visitors: Larry Bowman, Brad Gier, Joe Dentice, Chris Miller, Jeff Popple, Breanna, Skip and Diane, Chris Heinold, Brad Rogers and Paul Rose from the Gow School and on and on.

"It's been a busy morning," I said to Corinne.

My beautiful sister looked down away from me for a moment, but when she turned back, the tears that were glistening in her eyes were almost too much for me to handle.

"Did you ever meet anyone that didn't love him?" she asked.

"That person doesn't exist," I said.

Corinne bowed her head. I was glad that we were alone for a few moments.

"Did you know that little bastard calls our house every Saturday morning just to wake us up? And if we don't answer he doesn't stop calling, and he doesn't even have anything to say! He just wants to make sure we're all right. He just wants to shoot the shit!"

Corinne tried hard to stifle the tears, but I couldn't help her do it. We both wiped our eyes at the same time. "He's going to be okay," I said.

"He's gotta be."

I struggled to read the words contained in the notebook as Corinne sipped her own coffee and looked blankly at the television screen. She wasn't much interested in the program, though, because the volume was turned way too low for her to hear the dialogue. All at once, she laughed.

"What?" I asked.

"Do you remember when I dressed the two of you up for that Halloween party?"

I laughed along with her. "Yeah, classic Jeff," I said.

Together Corinne and I sat in the quiet waiting room, piecing the story together.

"He'd been calling me all day," I said. "After about the third time he called, I knew I'd have to go, but I still tried to protest. 'I'm not going,' I said.

"Sure you are," Jeff had said to me. "It's all set up. Brad, Hemer, Pops and Livecchi are holding the party and I already paid for you to get in."

Corinne smiled at the thought of Jeff manipulating me. I continued with the story as if the conversation had just taken place.

"Why would you pay for me?" I asked him. "I told you yesterday that I wasn't going."

"And I didn't believe you," Jeff had said. "Now please get in the car and meet me at Corinne's. Her and Chuck are going to dress us in their costumes. Remember, brother, life is a party, let's get out and participate!"

"What am I dressing up as?" I asked. I was already smiling with the thought of all that he had planned for me.

"My woman," he said.

Before I could even formulate an answer to such a statement, the line went dead. I took a deep breath. He was just so insufferable when he put his mind to something. I drove the twenty miles from my apartment to my sister's home, smiling at the thought that he never knew exactly what his day would bring to him. I had no way of knowing that it would be an evening that I would never forget, but I'm sure that Jeff had a sneaking suspicion of such. After all, he was all about creating memories, and he was always ready to bring me along for the ride.

If there is anything I can say disparaging about my

older sister Corinne, it's just that she fed the celebration machine that was Jeffrey. She loved to coax him toward a higher level of entertainment. Doing so was a dangerous proposition, but Corinne was willing to go the extra mile.

That Halloween evening both Corinne and Jeff were hitting on all cylinders. I nursed a beer with Chuck, and we watched the wheels turn as Corinne and Jeff hand-made the costumes that they promised would win us first place at the party.

Corinne worked on Jeff first. She ripped a pair of his pants just perfectly so that he was wearing just a brown loincloth-type of garment that showed about three feet of his legs and just a wee bit of his flat ass cheeks. He kept making Corinne cut it shorter, and one of the more comical moments came when he stepped too close to Chuck.

"Are you kidding me?" Chuck asked. "Get your ass out of my face!"

Corinne carefully painted white and red streaks on Jeff's face and fitted his nose with a huge clip-on earring. She slathered baby oil all over his body, gagging and laughing as she did so. Together they fashioned a spear out of a broom handle and a makeshift arrow. By the time I had finished my second beer, my partner was dressed to go.

"You're his wife," Corinne announced.

Chuck was looking on in horror. Jeff was practicing his war dance around their kitchen table.

"You're in for this?" Chuck asked in disbelief.

"What am I going to do?" I couldn't help but laugh.

I sat in the chair as Corinne fitted me with a blouse, made up my face, and painted my fingernails red. She also put a good coat of baby oil on me, making a joke of each dab. I stood and pirouetted as they examined my costume.

"It's good," Jeff said. "He makes an absolutely hideous

woman, but he's missing the cavewoman element. He needs more."

Corinne and Jeff left the room as I sat beside Chuck, who was content to look at me every few seconds, whistle and laugh. "You're a couple of real idiots," he said over and over.

Moments later Corinne and Jeff emerged from the bathroom. Corinne quickly added my own nose ring, which brought instant discomfort, but it was the small wicker basket that Jeff was holding that had me curious.

"What're you going to do with that?" I asked.

Without so much of a warning Jeff handed the basket to Corinne who slammed it down over the top of my head. My melon understandably broke through the bottom of the basket, and I cried out in pain.

"Perfect!" Jeff said. "There's my bush-woman!"

"Holy shit!" Chuck cried out as tears of laughter raced down his face.

I immediately jumped from the table and ran toward the full-length mirror in the bathroom. Corinne and Jeff peered over my shoulder as I took in the sight of the most ugly woman ever created.

Three hours later Jeff and I were awarded the first-place prize in a costume party that attracted nearly a hundred people. Yet it wasn't the bottle of booze that we proudly drank that offered me a memory that will never fade. Rather, it was the sight of watching Jeff race through the hall of people with his loincloth flapping, his right hand spanking his own ass cheeks, as he led the gathering in a karaoke singing of the Village People song, YMCA.

On a night when I wanted no part of his antics, I laughed as hard as I had ever laughed in my life. Why waste even a single day?

"He makes me laugh harder than anyone I've ever

met," Corinne said.

"I know," I said, "and what I wouldn't do to have him running around this room with his ass cheeks out, doing the YMCA dance."

Corinne bowed her head for a long moment. When she raised her crying eyes to me once more, she flashed a glance of determination that shot straight to my heart. "We have to get him through this," she said.

Her next sentence was about what needed to be done, right now. "Thanks for doing the night shift, Cliffy, we need someone with him all the time. Jim blew up your air mattress and wrote something in the book. Make sure you read that." She buttoned up her coat and flipped a red scarf around her neck. "Is it cold out there?"

"Brutal," I said. "Get some rest."

Corinne was spearheading a trip to Lynn's that would include dinner and helping Lynn with the kids.

"I won't be in for a little while," she said. "Call me with updates."

"You got it," I said.

Corinne stepped into the hallway. Leaving the hospital was almost as difficult as being there, and I stood up to watch her make the 10-step walk to the bank of elevators.

"Oh, Terrie Prime sent a tin of cookies," she said. "They're on the table next to your friend, the Pepsi machine. The cookies are just awesome, by the way."

"Excellent!" I said. "We definitely need something to go with all the coffee."

"Take care of him, Cliffy," Corinne said as she stepped into the elevator.

I headed back to the room. The Pepsi machine was mocking me with its aggravating hum. I ignored it for the moment, grabbed two chocolate chip cookies courtesy of the best baker in North Collins, and opened the notebook. I focused on Jim's words, scribbled neatly into the notebook. Those unbelievable words would carry the pain of the next few hours.

Jeff, I've been sitting here, hour after hour and day after day, trying to figure out how to help you, and I can't. For the first time, I can't. I wish that it were as easy as twisting a few screws for you like when I fixed your patio door. You can believe that if I could, I'd switch spots with you in a heartbeat. So much is running through my mind, but what comes back to me is you, my little brother. You have always helped me and been by my side, even when you thought that I was a little crazy. You are my best man, and the reason for that is not just because you are family, but also because you're a great guy, period! Hey, when you feel like you're at the end of your rope, call. I can fix a lot, and if I can't, I'll go through it with you. You have a lot of people sitting here, praying for you. You have three little people at home depending on you. If you need anything, just call. I'd go to the end of the earth for you, pal. I love you! Jim.

Chapter IV – The Promise

January 31, 2009 Faith is being sure of what we hope for and certain of what we do not see. Hebrews 11:1

The air mattress was just a tad more comfortable than the floor. I settled onto my pillow, fatigue finally hammering away at my pounding head and working its way through the caffeine haze.

Family friend John Cataldo had spent the evening with me, watching the Sabres game and delivering a bag of food that included salty snacks and high-powered drinks. Jeff was still heavily sedated and would once more sleep through the night, but John and I were wide awake and trying to solve the problems of life that seemed to be weighing heavily on our minds.

Just a few years before, John and his wife, Mary, had lost their daughter Heather to a malignant brain tumor. They had been forced to continue on with their beautiful girls Emily and Melissa, but would they ever find joy again?

"You never get over it," John said. "You get on with it."

John had left at midnight. His words were ringing in my ears. I was certain that if this didn't work out the way that I needed it to that I would neither get over it nor get on with it. Instinctively, despite my anger, I thought of God. If He was there, He was going to hear from me tonight.

When Jake was sick, Corinne had given me a finger rosary. I fingered the very same rosary that had once brought me a miracle and began saying Hail Marys one after another, reciting the words as the nuns had taught them to us. I drifted toward sleep, but two church-related memories forced my eyes to remain open.

One of the more consistent aspects of our lives up to that point was that, as practicing Roman Catholics, we were all expected to include our faith in everything we did. While our Catholic school upbringing played a huge role in the formation of our beliefs, as a family we also understood that the greatest of all commandments was actually our guiding force. We treated others as we wanted to be treated.

Jeff's formative years were a testament to this very commandment, and even if he didn't sing the loudest in church or wave a flag for others to see, he certainly believed, with his whole heart, that Jesus Christ was his savior. It was a belief that was fostered and nurtured by the man and woman who taught us faith. As with everything else in our lives, Mom and Dad were front and center, nudging us in the right direction.

Where the church was positioned in our lives was crystal clear to us during the early 1990s, when the Buffalo Bills ruled the American Conference of the football world, going to the Super Bowl a record four years in a row. Like everyone else in western New York, we were certainly caught up in football fever, and getting a ticket to the game was of utmost importance.

One Sunday morning the plans were all made, the car was packed for the tailgate party and as a group we could not be stopped, or so we thought.

"When did you two go to church?" Mom asked as Jeff and I sat at the breakfast table.

"Last week," Jeff said. He arched his eyebrows and smiled.

Mom scowled faintly.

"We'll go twice next week," Jeff tried again. Once more he raised his eyebrows as though he were Groucho Marx.

Again his joke was met with silence.

"Be serious, Mom" I said. "We're meeting everyone at the stadium at ten-thirty. Mass doesn't even start until eleven."

Once more Mom remained silent. I glanced at Jeff. I saw anguish on his face.

"Do what you need to do," Mom said, finally. "But I think if you have eight hours for football you should have at least an hour for God."

We headed for the car. Thinking about the "must" game the Bills were about to play, I certainly had no desire to spend an hour in church.

"What're we going to do?" I asked as Jeff backed the car out of the driveway.

"We're going to church," he said. "I'm not disappointing her."

So just as we had done every Sunday of our lives, we went to church.

Just a few short months later we were back at church once more. Mass at Holy Spirit ended just before noon. Jeff was piloting the car when he turned to my mother and asked if she'd like to go to breakfast.

"Yeah, let's go," I said from the back seat. "There's a place in Eden that serves breakfast all day."

My mother agreed and so instead of returning home we made the 10-mile jaunt to the town of Eden. I ordered steak and eggs and was just about done sopping up the last of the eggs with a piece of rye toast when I broke the news that I hadn't brought a dime to help pay the bill.

"I don't have any money either," my mother said with a laugh.

"I'm paying for everything?" Jeff asked.

My mother and I shared a long laugh at Jeff's expense.

"What's more," my mother said, "is that you need to lend me five bucks so I can grab a gallon of milk."

Jeff opened his wallet and extracted two twenty-dollar

bills.

"This is all I have for the week," he said. "I can't believe you're sticking me with the bill."

"You knew the risks," I said as my mother and I laughed once more.

"Laugh it up," Jeff said.

He was painfully quiet as he drove us to the Wilson Farms store for the gallon of milk. Jeff was just 18 years old, and he was working hard for his money, but Mom and I were just having a little fun with him. We would most certainly pay him back. He handed over the change from breakfast to my mother, and since we were having such a good time at Jeff's expense, I decided to join my mother during her trip through the store. "We'll be right back," I said. "I want to make sure Mom spends every nickel."

We spent just a few minutes in the store, and I was a little giddy over the fact that we'd played a joke on the world's biggest practical joker. I held the door for my mother as she stepped outside into the completely empty parking lot.

"What the hell?" my mother asked.

"He left us," I said.

"He wouldn't do that," my mother said.

"Where is he then?" I asked. "And this is Jeff we're talking about. He'd do it in a heartbeat."

"We're ten miles from home!"

Deep in my heart I figured that Jeff had taken a quick trip around the block to scare us a little.

"He was pissed about us stiffing him for breakfast," I said.

"I'm his mother. He's going to leave his mother to walk home ten miles?"

We started off down the road. Traffic was light on Route 62, and there was no sign of Jeff. Thankfully, about a half-mile into the trip our good friend, Chris Heinold, passed us going the other way. He pulled to the side of the road and was completely baffled by what he was seeing.

"Mrs. Fuzz, why in God's name are you walking?" Chris asked.

"Jeff left us," my mother said. "I'm thinking he's coming back, but he was aggravated because we made him pay for breakfast."

"He isn't coming back," Chris said. "I just passed by him. He's already in North Collins." When Chris pulled into our driveway, sure enough Jeff's car was in the yard.

"You left me in Eden to walk home?" my mother asked Jeff when she saw him.

"Laugh it up," he said.

***

Recalling these stories forced me to sit up on the air mattress. My mother so enjoyed Jeff's jokes, his nearly constant smile and the fact that he would travel to the end of the Earth for her if she asked him to. Years and years later Mom and Jeff laughed about how he'd left her so far away from home. "I knew Chris would pick you guys up," he confessed.

I tried hard to get into a comfortable position. I debated unplugging the Pepsi machine, fluffed my pillow and glanced at the time on the face of my cell phone, 12:30 a.m. I needed sleep. I put the rosary into the pocket of my sweatpants, punched the pillow with my right hand and felt the air mattress shift with my weight. Everything about everything just plain sucked.

I don't recall drifting off, but in the end it didn't matter much anyway; I slept peacefully for just over fifty minutes. The overhead light in the waiting room had snapped on causing me to bolt straight up.

"Hey there's a homeless dude here," a young man in a

blue gown shouted.

"I'm not homeless," I said. "My brother's in the ICU."

"It's just funny to see someone sleeping on the floor," he said. Another man joined him and together they laughed at me.

"Yeah, it's a real funny-fucking-joke," I said.

The two idiots were heading toward the Pepsi machine. It didn't occur to them, even for a second, that turning out the light might be the Christian thing to do, so I returned the favor. I didn't say a single word about the non-working Pepsi machine. I watched it eat the guy's dollar.

"Hey, it ain't working," the guy said to me as though I might find it in my heart to refund the money for him.

"It worked earlier," I said. "Try a clean dollar."

Stupidly, he put in another dollar and the Pepsi machine, which I was considering in a whole new light, ate it as well.

"That sucks!" his partner exclaimed.

"Yeah, it's a real tragedy," I said.

They turned out the light and shuffled down the hall, guffawing about the fact that they'd found a homeless man in their waiting room.

Sleep was out of the question. I picked the air mattress off the floor, turned on the television and found Happy Gilmour playing on TBS.

"That'll work," I said, but there were a couple of things I had to do first.

I shuffled down the long, lonely hallway. I placed my right hand under the sanitizer container and punched down on the pump. The scent of the alcohol reached my nose as I rubbed my hands together. I punched the wall button and stepped into the darkened ICU.

To my surprise, the lights were on in Jeff's room. A nurse was by his bedside, struggling to move Jeff in the bed. She appeared to be cleaning him, and as I watched from just inside the door, her name came to me. "Hi, Carolyn," I said.

All at once Jeff shifted in the bed. He appeared to be agitated. His right leg came off the bed, and he held it in the air.

"Wow, he's moving a lot," I said.

"Tell me about it," Carolyn said, "and he's a strong man. He's starting to get a little aggravated with everything."

"Him and me both," I said.

Carolyn was a short, quick-moving woman, and she whizzed by me and out into the hall.

I stood beside Jeff, taking his left hand in my right. "How about a squeeze?" I asked.

Jeff's eyes were open. He seemed to be looking right through me.

"He isn't squeezing with his left hand," Carolyn said as she motored back into the room, "but he gave me a heck of a squeeze with his right."

The words were music to my heart. It was certainly progress!

"He's sedated tonight, but tomorrow they plan on cutting back on the meds a bit, so we may see more activity."

"A little at a time," I said. Inside I was jumping for joy. Despite the fatigue and my aggravation with the two men who'd barged into my sleeping quarters, I was thrilled with Jeff's movements and the fact that there were women like Carolyn in the world.

"That's right," Carolyn said. "It's a long haul, but he'll get there. You're sleeping in the waiting room, right?"

"Sleeping is a shaky way to put it," I said, "but, yeah, our family is here around the clock. I'm sure you've seen a few guys and gals who look like me roaming the halls. We all have the dark hair and brown eyes although most of my hair has left."

Carolyn smiled. "The love of your family will get Jeff through," she said. "That and prayers, plenty of prayers."

Jeff's eyes were slowly closing. I held his hand for a few moments more. I wished he was sitting up with me watching the movie, and I quickly recalled that we'd seen Tommy Boy together two nights in a row because it had made us laugh. "Rest well, my brother," I whispered, and I made the lonely walk back toward the waiting room.

Of course, there was one more stop that needed to be made. I punched the button for the elevator, fished through my pockets for change and mindlessly stood in front of the coffee machine in the deserted cafeteria. I didn't even have to consider the options. I punched in IA6, and the coffee started to flow into a small cup with an ace of diamonds on the side.

"Yeah, like I feel like playing fucking poker," I said.

The cup filled and I put another dollar into the slot. There was no sense in just getting one cup. My new container had a seven of clubs.

Back in the waiting room, Adam Sandler was involved in a classic fight with Bob Barker. Despite the fact that it was 3:20 a.m. a few days into the worst time in my life, I laughed when Sandler shouted, "The price is wrong, Bob!"

"You love this part," I whispered as though Jeff were seated right beside me.

He had always been right beside me. I thought of the fact that he was starting to move around in that bed. Would he be able to laugh with me again? Would he pull practical joke after practical joke on me again? With Happy Gilmour running around the golf course, I remembered what had to be one of the greatest pranks that he'd ever pulled on me.

During our formative years and well into our twenties,

we played pickup basketball three times a week. On one such night I returned home from work to find Jeff waiting for me at my apartment door. He had made the calls to get the group to play. Yet that night, I was tired and I was debating not even making the trip out.

"Let's go, Moe," Jeff yelled as I got out of my car. "You're driving. Dad made macaroni and peas. We're eating and playing. You don't even have time to put your crap away."

"Dude, I can't just get up and go. I need to run to the store for a minute." Without too much thought, I decided to go, as Jeff's encouragement was contagious and I never, ever could turn down my father's macaroni and peas.

"Hurry up," Jeff yelled. "I'll wait here. Give me the apartment key."

"Don't steal anything," I said as I tossed him the key.

Fifteen minutes later, we were in my car, listening to Bob Dylan, making the half-hour drive. Jeff was in prime form, laughing, making fun of my quickly declining basketball skills and smiling from ear to ear. All at once it dawned on me. He had the look of someone who had sabotaged my living quarters.

"What did you do in my apartment?" I asked.

"You'll find out soon enough," he replied devilishly.

I was distracted all the way through my macaroni and peas. As we played ball, I shot the basketball horribly because each and every time down the court Jeff would look in my direction and laugh. It was all I could do just to concentrate. I needed to get back to the apartment and find the havoc that he created.

A few hours later we were back in the apartment complex driveway. Jeff still hadn't owned up to what he had done in my apartment when I left him alone for just fifteen minutes.

"Are you coming in to see the anguish when I figure out what you did?" I asked.

"Oh no," Jeff replied. "That's the sheer brilliance of this joke. It's going to pay off for a long time."

Turning the key in the apartment door I was in a state of sheer panic. Two steps into the door I realized that he had not ransacked the place. Everything appeared to be in perfect order, just as I had left it. I looked through my desk drawers, the bureau drawers, in the top deck of the toilet, everywhere. There didn't seem to be one thing out of place. I telephoned Jeff to ask what he had done, but he wasn't talking.

"You'll figure it out," he said. "Consider it my little puzzle to you."

That night, sleep was troublesome. I racked my brain trying to solve the puzzle and finally fell asleep, still caught up in his little game.

The next morning, I got out of bed early thinking about my day, nearly forgetting the turmoil of his little joke. I opened the door to my pantry and nearly fell to my knees in front of the cupboard.

Jeff had removed every label from the generous cupboard full of canned goods. Each can looked exactly the same. I grabbed the telephone. "You bastard!" I said just after he yelled his hello.

"Think of the beauty of it," he answered. "A few weeks from now, feeling that you'd really like a bowl of soup, you're going to open up a nice can of peaches."

"There's something wrong with you," I said. I was trying hard to stifle a laugh.

"You gotta admit that's a good one," Jeff said.

"Yeah, thanks."

By the way, he had been exactly right. Just about a month into the little joke, I threw out a can of French-style green beans. I had wanted soup. Those 15 minutes he spent alone in my apartment haunted me for a long time.

Back in the waiting room, Happy Gilmour gave way to European Vacation. I wasn't much into watching Chevy Chase bumble and stumble his way around Europe, so I headed back to Jeff's room. He was resting well, but his right leg was off the bed; he looked as though he were just a couple of moves from jumping down to the floor. I held his left hand for what seemed like an hour. "Who's better than you?" I asked him. It was a line that we'd shared for the last few years. "Dude, I promise you I'm going to do everything possible to make sure that you're okay."

The one-sided conversation wasn't doing much for me. I was on the verge of an absolute breakdown. The caffeine was racing through my veins. The morning light was breaking, and I knew that Chuck and John would soon be there to send me off to sleep.

"I promise," I whispered. "Nobody's better than you. I promise."

Chapter V – Glory Days

January 31 & February 01, 2009 Do not give into sad-ness; torment not yourself with brooding; gladness of heart is the very life of man. Cheerfulness prolongs his days. Distract yourself, renew your courage; drive resent-ment far away from you; for worry has brought death to many, nor is there aught to be gained from resentment. Anonymous.

In the middle of the night on the 31st of January I had my first real conversation with Jeff since he'd been strick-en. "Can you get me some water?" he asked.

"I can't," I said.

"Come on, don't break my balls," he said.

I held his right hand.

"Squeeze my hand," I said.

Jeff frowned and I felt the pressure as he squeezed. "Give me some water," he begged.

"I don't know where it is," I said.

Jeff motioned with his head toward the sink in the back corner of the room. His eyes were wide open. I wondered if he saw the tears of happiness welling in my eyes. He was awake! He was speaking! He was following com-mands! "Water," he said again.

We had been instructed not to do anything, and there wasn't any way that I was about to give him water if he wasn't supposed to have it.

"I don't know how to get it," I said.

"Turn the faucet on," he whispered. "Call Sam, he'll do it for me."

My heart was singing at the mere mention of my boy's name. Not only was Jeff awake and sharing, he was remembering!

"Are you going to get me water?" he asked.

"I can't," I said.

"Then get out," he answered.

I all but ran from the room to the waiting room where I wrote the exchange in the green notebook. "He's wide awake! He's talking! He told me not to break his balls!"

God is on our side! my brain screamed to me. Day after day he would get better. It would take time, but he would be back, leading the parade in no time at all.

On Saturday morning I headed for home after another long night on the hospital waiting room floor. John and Jim relieved me for the long day shift, and I hustled toward home so that Kathy could take Jake to his basketball game while Sam stayed around the house with me. I was dead tired but a long way from sleep because for the first time, Jeff was showing signs of battling back. We were all buoyed by Jeff's rally, as he was tossing and turning in the bed, trying hard to communicate and moving everything on his right side. I was happy to hand the baton to John and Jim and see the kids for a little while.

But as I drove the five miles to our home, I couldn't tear my eyes away from the early morning sky. The low-hanging, dark clouds gave the sky a gun powder-gray look, and the fact that I was looking up reminded me of a night I'd spent with Jeff.

In August of 1995 there was also another reason to celebrate within the Fazzolari family. Carrie was preparing to start law school in Dayton, Ohio, and there wasn't any way that we could let her get on the road without a proper send-off. Once more we gathered at our parents' home in North Collins where we shared a big meal and a few beers. As the party wound down, I headed out into the front yard with Jeff beside me. He stopped me in my tracks as he glanced skyward.

"Do you ever think about how beautiful life is?" he asked.

"What the hell are you talking about?" I asked.

"Look up, dude," he said.

The stars were burning bright in the black void. Jeff was holding a beer in his hand, but it was all but forgotten as he studied the night sky. "Days like today are just so perfect," he said. "We're doing good, aren't we?"

"Yeah it's pretty perfect," I said. I still wasn't exactly sure what he was talking about, but he was so thoughtful about it I thought I'd play along.

"Andrea and Nicole are beautiful," he said. He was speaking of John and Dana's children, and in the darkness I clearly saw the twinkle in his eye. Perhaps it was the bright stars that allowed me to see it.

"And Carrie, man, she's always had it together."

We clanked beer bottles and headed back to the party. The message had been clear. The love that was filling his heart was all for our family. There was no getting around the fact that he was sharing in John and Carrie's accomplishments. He was gazing at the stars, knowing that, in some way, it was all connected.

"I love looking up," Jeff said. "People should look up more."

***

As I pulled into my driveway, I kept my eyes on the low-hanging clouds in the early morning sky. I wasn't about to exclaim life was beautiful, though. I was struggling with the idea that life was moving on despite the fact that we were in the middle of an ominous tug of war between life and death.

Jeff had made it through the seventy-two hours that the doctors had deemed the most dangerous time, and the fact that they were bringing him around was enough to keep my spirits up, at least a little.

I rushed through a nap and then watched a couple of comedy shows with Jake, Matthew and Sam. We settled down for dinner as we did each and every night, but this time I cherished the moments and encouraged the lively banter that only children can provide. We were about halfway through dinner when Jake made a special request. "Can you tell the story about Aunt Dana and Frank?"

I knew exactly what Jake was talking about, but I looked to Kathy for support. I was on such an emotional brink I wasn't sure that I could speak of Jeff as though we were going to be left with just the memories.

"Yeah, tell it, tell it," Sam said.

I shook my head as Kathy smiled, but I knew that I was going to have to cheer the kids up. They were unsure of what was going on, and they loved their uncle so much that perhaps the story would do some good.

"Years and years ago, Aunt Dana was backing up the car when our dog, Frank, wandered behind it. Frank didn't make it, but it was so heartbreaking for Aunt Dana that no one ever talked about it happening or even mentioned Frank."

Jake and Matt had already heard the story, but they were on the edge of the chair waiting for the punchline.

"A lot of years passed without anyone ever speaking of Frank, but one Sunday the entire family was gathered around the dinner table. Meatballs were flying off the plates and the crushed red pepper was being passed from hand to hand. Jeff figured that things were too quiet so he brought up Frank's name."

"I remember!" Jake said. "He was telling me about Frank."

"Yes," I said. "He told you that we had a dog named Frank, and that we all really, really loved Frank. Aunt Dana got up from the table and walked away. Uncle John tried to get Uncle Jeff to stop talking about it, but it was already too late."

Sam hadn't heard the end of the story, so I took my time in telling it.

"Jake asked Uncle Jeff what happened to Frank, and the entire room went quiet. Uncle John was begging Jeff not to say anything about the accident, and Aunt Dana didn't even look at him. Uncle Jeff wiped the corners of his mouth, winked at Uncle John, and in his Boris Karloff voice said, 'Frank was murdered!'"

The kids all laughed.

"I can just see him doing that," Matt said.

"Was Aunt Dana mad?" Jake asked.

"Not long," I said. "Aunt Dana knows Jeff after all these years. I think she even laughed about it later, but it was just Jeff's way of telling her that it was okay and that we still loved her."

The boys took turns doing the "Frank was murdered" line over and over, but Jake's pointed question stopped me dead in my tracks. "Is he going to be all right?"

"He'll be fine," I said. "But we need to pray for him really hard because he's pretty sick, and it's going to take awhile."

Jake, who barely remembered his personal fight for life, brought the subject up for me to consider. "You guys were real worried when I was in the hospital, and look at me, I'm fine."

"Exactly!" I said. "But you guys are going to have to help us too because me and Mom are going to be spending a lot of time at the hospital. You'd do that for your brother, right?"

"Not Sam," Jake joked.

"Yeah, you would," I said. "Now go play a game so me and Mom can talk for awhile."

The boys scattered to other areas of the house as

Kathy and I tried to work out the schedule for the remainder of the evening. Sleeping on the floor was beginning to take a toll, and while I would never complain and didn't want to do it any other way, I couldn't hide my fatigue from Kathy.

"Why don't I head up there for awhile?" Kathy asked. "I can sit with Jeff for a few hours, and you can relax. Come on up by ten or so."

"I guess," I said. "But he's been so much more awake. I hate being there and I hate being away."

"Corinne said the same exact thing to me today," Kathy said. "But you guys all have to rely on each other, right? Jeff's in good hands whether he's with you, me, Lynn, or John, or Corinne, or Jim or Carrie. Everyone loves him. No one is just going to leave him there alone."

"I know." I said. I was on the verge of tears once more. Kathy opened her arms and I pulled her into a deep hug.

"I'll head up there and call you with an update," she said. "Try to relax."

I sat in front of the television, not hearing so much as a single word of the program that was playing. My mind was like a reel-to-reel player as I recalled day after day after day after day. I couldn't escape the fact that John and Jim had spent the entire day at Jeff's side and that they were every bit as torn apart as I was. We'd spent so many moments just being brothers.

At just eleven years old it was becoming painfully apparent to all of us that Jeff was soon to become the best athlete in the family. Perhaps spurred on by his brother's love of competition, Jeff could already shoot a basketball as well as any of us, and despite the fact that he was tall and rail thin, he was quite ready for the challenge of mixing it up in a two-on-two match up that was ready-made.

The standard game always pitted John and Jeff against Jim and me. The match-up was fairly even because Jim never felt much like running, and I was often guarded by John, who would rather foul hard than play regular defense.

On one particular afternoon, the game started with Jim and me controlling the ball. Jim took the pass, saw that he couldn't shoot over Jeff's long arms, and passed it to me. I went up for the shot. With arms fully extended, I took aim for the basket, and John threw a punch that caught me just under the breastbone, knocking me to the ground, gasping for breath.

"My foul," John said.

"What're you doing?" I asked.

"I fouled you," John answered.

"Why would you punch me?" I asked with tears in my eyes as the ball bounced aimlessly at my feet.

"So you think about it the next time you go up for a shot," John said.

The tone for the game was set from that very first moment, and then Jeff took over. His long arms, quick feet and jumping ability took control, and with John acting as his thug and bodyguard, Jeff scored from all angles.

The games normally concluded with one brother or another storming off the court, but hours later, at Jeff's urging we would be back at it, playing game after game until the sun went down.

One hot, August day with the score tied and the cry going out that the next basket would win, Jeff moved with the ball toward the goal. He raised his left arm to release the game-winning shot, and I blocked it, retrieved the ball and quickly scored. Walking from the court, I tried to school Jeff.

"Next time you're in that position give a pump fake," I said. "Just pretend you're going to shoot, wait for the defender to go by and then release it."

Jeff nodded, but left the court disappointed just the

same. Three days later, Jeff pump-faked me high into the air, turned the corner and banked in a lay-up to win the game.

"Thanks for the move," he said.

"What're brothers for?" I asked.

My relaxing evening at home drew to a close by nine p.m. I said prayers with the boys, kissed them goodnight and called Kathy to let her know that I was on my way back to the hospital to take over for her. She answered her cell phone on the first ring.

"Jeff just gave me the finger," she said.

"Come on!" I said.

"He did! He's been pretty awake this evening, and when I walked in the room, he flipped me off."

My heart was doing a dance. If he recognized Kathy and was teasing her already, he'd be back with us in no time. Tears were stinging my eyes, and I looked to the sky as I drove. Thank you, God!

"You don't have to rush," Kathy said. "He's had a ton of visitors today, and I'm still sitting here with Jim and John."

"Jim and John?" I asked. "They were there at eight-thirty this morning."

Kathy laughed. "Yeah, they can't leave either. All of you are going to end up getting sick. Jeff's going to be better and his five brothers and sisters are going to be in bed for a month."

I parked the car and all but ran into the hospital. I needed to see Jeff awake, alert and flipping people off.

My excitement was short-lived, however because by the time I reached Jeff's room, he was resting again. I sat for a few minutes with John, Jim and Kathy, but before long, they left me alone in that quiet of the waiting room.

Much later that night, in my spot in the back corner of the ICU waiting room, a couple of things dawned on me. First and foremost was that the room was becoming something of a pigsty. There were snack crumbs on the ugly brown carpet, and the only garbage can in the place was filled with discarded coffee cups. And secondly, the mattress was just about out of air.

I sat up and kicked the Buffalo Bills blanket off my legs. The Pepsi machine was still making noises as if there were a plane landing in the room, but I didn't mind it so much after it had kicked out my intruders the night before.

I considered what was right there in front of us. The room could be vacuumed in the morning, Jim could re-inflate the mattress and I would eventually get some rest. All was definitely not lost because for the first time in five days I actually believed in my heart that Jeff would be just fine. His parade of visitors had been treated to one hell of a show during the day. Jeff had flipped Kathy off, had chatted briefly with John and Jim, recognized that his pal Jeff Popple was there and had visited with his buddy Mike and Mike's wife Carla.

I fluffed the pillow and lay back down on the mattress, which made a groaning sound underneath me. My plan had been to rest for an hour and then get back to the room to see if Jeff were also awake. His periods of rest were getting shorter, and if his eyes were open, I wanted to be with him. Yet sleep wouldn't come.

I gathered the Bills blanket that my old college friends Lisa and Frank Zocco had sent me years ago, turned on an old episode of Married with Children and sat in one of the hard plastic chairs in an effort to further survey the scene. The comfort conditions of the waiting room were actually deplorable. In the five days we'd been there not one person had visited to clean the room. My sisters had gathered the garbage and actually had made the call for it to be emptied, but the coffee cups were hanging over the lid. To top it off, I'd slept on the floor for four straight nights and not one person had offered me even as much as a cup of coffee.

"The whole thing's a fucking mess," I muttered to my-self.

I picked up the green notebook and began scanning what had happened as I'd rested at home. Corinne had led a charge with my cousin Paul's wife, Linda, to help Lynn out at the house. The work detail, which included Dana and my beautiful nieces Andrea and Nicole, had helped with the kids, prepared a meal and cleaned up a bit.

Carrie's stay had also been extended as her children Paige and Tony made the trip up from Baltimore due to a great assist by our cousin Aimee Switala, who'd flown with the kids, handed them off at the Buffalo airport to Carrie and immediately returned to Baltimore.

Al Bundy was up to his usual crap on the television, but my mind really was elsewhere. I continued paging through the book, taking in the names of the visitors. Larry Bowman and Nancy, Noel and Alex, Tony Colan-tino, Scott Weiser, Jim, Lisa, and nephew James and Lisa's parents George and Joann.

"So much love."

With the thought of love hammering away at my tat-tered brain I couldn't help but think of my mother and father. They had devoted every ounce of their strength to make sure that we were a family that stayed tight through thick and thin. Leading by example, my parents had pro-vided each of us children with a strong work ethic and a well-defined understanding of what it was to cherish life within a family.

"That's all Jeff wants, too," I whispered. "God, please help my brother raise his family."

I closed the notebook as tears threatened me. What was I doing? This had been a great day. I kicked the deflated air mattress to the corner and headed down the hallway. I sure hoped that Jeff were awake.

At one-thirty in the morning my conversation with Jeff was rather one-sided, but he was wide awake. He gave me the finger when I walked into the room, and I smiled. My smile dimmed as his hand moved to the tube on his nose. I saw that his hand had been restrained. I was considering the restraint when Carolyn cleared her throat as she entered the room.

"He's been bad," Carolyn said. "He's ripping at the tube."

I certainly didn't want him to reach any of the tubes, but I was glad that he was fighting back. Jeff looked at me, sighed heavily, and dropped his arm to his side, his attempt at getting to the tube over for a moment.

"Crazy," he groaned out.

"What?" I asked, leaning a little closer.

"Just crazy," Jeff answered.

My heart did a little leap in my chest. He was aware of what was going on! It was crazy, but we would make it through.

"You need to keep resting," I said. "It'll take awhile, but you'll be okay."

Jeff bowed his hand and deftly brought his hand toward his mouth. I thought that maybe he'd had an itch or something, and I was leaning forward to help, but Carolyn was more aware of what Jeff was trying to do.

"He's biting at the oxygen monitor on his finger," she said. "He wants all this off of him."

"You have to behave," I whispered.

"Oh, he's being bad," Carolyn said.

Jeff rolled his eyes and closed them. "You sound like my wife," he croaked.

I stayed at the bedside until 2:30a.m. Carolyn explained that they gave Jeff a bit more of the sedative and that he'd rest the remainder of the night. "You should sleep some, too," she said.

I shuffled back down the hall with my mind on making it to the morning. It was Super Bowl Sunday, and Bruce Springsteen would be providing the halftime entertainment.

Before dozing off to sleep, I considered that I wouldn't be sharing much of the game with Jeff, and that it would be strange. We had bet on nearly every football game for twenty-five years. Like everything else, football was an unshakeable bond. As I settled into position in the waiting room I considered the weekends I had shared with Jeff.

Each and every Sunday morning the telephone would ring sometime between 7 a.m. and 9 a.m. In the days before caller ID, I knew that Jeff was calling with his football picks.

Over the course of twenty-five years, Jeff and I would pick every football game with the spread. We alternated games as they were set on the line in the Sunday paper, and kept a running tally of dollars. Most games were worth one dollar, but each week we both chose a three-dollar game and a five-dollar game. From week to week, the competition was fierce. If Jeff were up at the end of the day on Sunday he would call again.

"You're so stooooopid," he would chide me.

If I were in the lead, I would make the teasing telephone call.

By the end of the year the running total was just an afterthought, and we were usually within just a few dollars of one another. Yet the dollar amount didn't matter, because whoever lost was required to buy dinner for the winner. In the early years, dinner usually consisted of a burger and fries. It was the losing that really stung.

Yet the bet changed as we grew to adults. In 2004, Jeff won the dinner by a single dollar. To pay my debt, I decided that we would head to Marco's, a wonderful Italian restaurant in Buffalo.

"We're bringing the families, right?" Jeff asked.

"Dude, I owe you a dollar!"

"Doesn't matter," Jeff said. "See you there."

Jeff ordered an appetizer with his meal. He also ordered soup, chicken nuggets for Johnny and Farrah, a plate of stuffed peppers and a glass of wine. Lynn also ordered a special type of wine and the most expensive dinner on the menu. Glancing at the menu I was shocked to see that the particular glasses of wine that they ordered ran about $20 apiece.

"This dinner is going to cost me over $300," I complained.

Jeff raised his glass in a toast. "That's because you're so stoooopid."

I was happy to pay the bill, though, because it was a meal filled with laughter as our children shared a long, wonderful evening.

The very next football season ended in a different manner. Our yearlong bet went down to the very last week and thankfully my team won the Super Bowl to leave me with a three-dollar edge.

"Where you taking me to dinner?" I asked.

I was dreaming of Marco's and payback on the expensive glasses of wine.

"Oh, I'm cooking dinner," he said. "Hot dogs and beans," Jeff replied.

Being that we had not completely spelled out the parameters of our bet, and struggling with the idea that Jeff was always all about the joke, I was a little nervous in allowing him to go that route. But much as I had done the year before, Jeff made it an evening to remember.

One Saturday in August, with my wife and kids out of the house for the day, Jeff telephoned. "I'm making your dinner tonight," he said.

"What's on the menu?" I asked.

"I'm not telling you. Just be here at five. Chris Miller and Jim are coming too."

"Whoa, wait a minute," I said. "This is my dinner. You can't shortchange me."

"You won't be shortchanged," he said, and without so much as a goodbye, the telephone line went dead.

I stopped talking and looked at the telephone. For one reason or another, I just didn't trust him. He had to have something up his sleeve.

I arrived promptly at five and was served a glass of red wine. Chris and Jim had already started in on their wine, but Jeff cautioned us.

"This isn't about drinking," he said. "You boys better be ready to eat."

A cucumber and tomato salad followed. It was served with fresh basil and Asiago cheese. A basket of warm garlic bread was placed in the center of the table and, piece by piece, it disappeared.

"I called Uncle Jim," Jeff said. "He said that he's going to try to make it but he has to eat dinner first."

We all laughed. Uncle Jim was a legend of sorts when it came to sharing good food, and we enjoyed his company immensely.

Next out of the kitchen was a full platter of Jeff's homemade stuffed banana peppers. Truth be told, it was the one item that I had insisted be on the menu. It had become sport to try the stuffed peppers in all of the restaurants in the Buffalo area. As I finished the first pepper of three, one thing was absolutely clear in my mind: there wasn't a single chef who prepared a stuffed pepper better than my brother.

Jeff grinned as he watched us eat. He rubbed his hands together excitedly. "Are you ready for the main course?" he asked.

"I'm about full now," I said.

Jeff refilled my wine glass. "Oh, my wonderful brother, you haven't even started yet."

Fortunately, the arrival of the main course was held up by the arrival of Uncle Jim. He immediately grabbed a seat beside me. "Sorry I'm late," he said. "Aunt Sherry got a pizza. I had to help her eat it."

"And now you're eating again?" Jeff asked.

"I only had two pieces," Uncle Jim said as he began to wolf down a couple of stuffed peppers and a piece of garlic bread.

The main course is hard to describe to someone who has never eaten until pain cripples you. Jeff had stuffed a-ten-pound beef tenderloin with crabmeat. The tenderloin was placed in the center of the table and cut perfectly even. Jeff placed a huge piece of meat on each plate, but stopped us before we were able to dig in.

"There's more," he said as he escaped into the kitchen. He returned with a huge bowl of pasta and a plate of steamed green beans with almond slices.

"Are you freaking kidding me?" Jim asked.

Jeff just laughed. "I'm paying off a three-dollar bet here," he said.

For the next twenty minutes, silence ruled the table. About three-quarters of the way through the meal, I began to feel a pain in my left side. I had never eaten so much food at a single sitting! As I put my fork into the last little morsel of meat on my plate, the pain in the side grew sharper and more pronounced.

"Look, guys, Cliff's eating himself into a coma," Jeff said.

By the time we were done, there was still enough food left on the table to feed a family of five. Uncle Jim offered the perfect ending prayer for a wonderful dinner.

"Anyone going to finish the tomato salad?" he asked.

"It's all yours," I said.

Reaching across the table, our beautiful uncle pulled the bowl toward him. "You're all a bunch of candy-asses," he said.

It's awfully difficult to forget the pure joy that Jeff felt on that day. He was never happier than when he was serving up his culinary creations to a group of people he loved.

Back at the hospital, in the middle of the present-day nightmare, sleep finally came for me just before three in the morning, but an emergency call over the loudspeaker woke me at a few minutes after four. I jumped off the nearly flat air mattress and shuffled down the hall to Jeff's room. What would I do if they were all in his room trying to bring him back from in an emergency situation? How could I help?

Before I could answer any of those questions, I was in Jeff's room, beside his bed. He was still fast asleep, and the commotion was taking place a few rooms away. I didn't even consider the other family fighting for one of their own. Jeff was all right. That was all I needed to know.

Family friend Chris Miller was the first to arrive on Sunday morning, but Corinne and Chuck, Jeff Popple and John quickly followed him.

"This is the first Sunday since he had teeth that he isn't going to eat pasta," Chuck said.

"Yeah, but he's starting to wake up," I said. "It shouldn't be too many Sundays that he goes without."

I filled in all the visitors on Jeff's activities of the night, and I saw the hope in their eyes as they envisioned him up and out of bed soon.

"He's still in for a hell of a fight," Chris explained. "The type of stroke he suffered is a bad one. It's a good thing he's such a strong man."

"He's battling though."

It was nearly eight-thirty in the morning when I made it home. Kathy and the boys were just waking up, but I wasn't going to be able to spend a lot of time with them. The need for sleep was overwhelming, and I would need the rest because I was planning on watching the Super Bowl at the hospital.

At home, I forced myself to stay awake for an hour or so as I talked with Matt, Jake and Sam, and tossed a ball for Shadow, our black Lab. By the time I made it to my bedroom, it was all I could do to take off my shoes before falling into bed.

I slept soundly for four hours, but upon waking I sat on the edge of the bed and realized that I'd been dreaming that I was asleep. For a brief moment I considered asking if someone else could handle the night shift, but I quickly dismissed the notion. The rest of the family was putting in long hours, too. This wasn't the time to go soft. I'd play my role.

Although Jeff wouldn't be having pasta today, the rest of the family certainly would be. I stirred the sauce, considering all of the Sunday feasts that we'd shared through the years. One particular Sunday stood out.

Growing up there was no mistaking what was going to transpire on a Sunday. As a family we would wake to the wonderful aroma of garlic and onion sautéing in olive oil. Dad was always at the stove, carefully stirring, cooking it slowly, making sure it was perfect every time. Every once in awhile one of the boys would be at his side, learning his tricks or helping to chop the onion into small pieces.

In November of 1978, I was the child at Dad's side for "the lesson."

"I'm thinking of doing tripe today," Dad said.

"What's tripe?" I asked.

"The stomach lining of a cow. It's delicious," Dad said.

I crinkled my nose. Dad had served tripe on a few other occasions and just the scent of it made me want to throw up. Tripe, as it is cooking can best be described as giving off the scent of burning tires. "Can I just have rigatoni?" I asked.

"I'll make both," Dad said. "I know John and Jim will eat tripe with me. Maybe Jeff will try it."

"I don't want any," I said.

On that Sunday morning, we all gathered around the table, eating meatballs from the sauce and talking about who might eat the tripe.

"I'm trying it," Jeff said.

"It's the best," John said. I wondered if he really liked tripe or was just trying to get in good with Dad.

The meatball breakfast was followed by a trip to church. Returning home, we all understood that it was quiet time, as Dad, who'd risen in the middle of the night, would take a nap. Before heading up to the bedroom, he turned the pot of tripe on low and instructed us to behave.

Twenty minutes later, I returned to the kitchen. Jeff was on a chair in front of the stove, wooden spoon in hand. The tripe now on high heat, was bubbling in the kettle on the stove.

"What're you doing?" I asked.

"Cooking the tripe," he said.

"You shouldn't touch that," I said.

Thankfully, Mom came upon the scene, returned the sauce to simmer and removed the spoon from Jeff's hand.

"I was just cooking," Jeff said. "I like cooking."

"You ruin his tripe and he's going to cook you," I told him.

It was too late. When Dad got up from his nap, he entered the kitchen and immediately said, "Someone scorched the sauce."

Mom explained what had happened, and even though Dad practiced a few Italian swear words, he took it fairly well. He set about trying to repair the damage, admonishing Jeff for trying to cook when he wasn't there.

At three o'clock on the button, dinner was served. I sat before a full dish of rigatoni, nearly gagging as the bowls of smelly tripe were handed out. John and Jim immediately dug in.

"Jeff, are you trying tripe or do you want pasta?" Dad asked.

"Tripe!" Jeff said.

I was skeptical. Dad was still smarting from the scorched sauce, but he dished out a bowl of tripe for his youngest son. "I don't want you to waste it," he said as he placed the bowl in front of Jeff.

"It's great," Jim said. "You're going to love it."

I wasn't so sure. I saw the look on Jeff's face. He picked up a piece of tripe and held it an inch from his nose. It looked to me as though he, too, were fighting a gag. Every eye was upon him as he put the tripe in his mouth.

"BLAH!" he screamed as he spat the tripe across the table. "That's awful!"

This time Dad wasn't quite so understanding. Still agitated by what had happened to the sauce, he loudly asked Jeff to leave the table. I watched him slink away as we all laughed at his first attempt to prepare a meal. It was to be the very last time that he ever botched a recipe.

Following dinner, still dreading the return to the hospital, I was on the couch watching the pre-game show for the Super Bowl when Sam entered the room. Despite the fact that Sam was just eight years old, he knew everything about the two teams involved.

"Arizona is going to win," he said. "Kurt Warner is awesome. He's going to light up the Steelers."

I patted the couch next to me and Sam sat down.

"I don't think so," I said. "Pittsburgh never loses in the Super Bowl."

Sam nuzzled close and it pained me that we weren't going to be watching the game together. Sam seemed to sense my discomfort.

"Did you bet with Uncle Jeff?" he asked.

"It's my pick," I said. "I'm taking Pittsburgh. I'll tell him when I get to the hospital. I have to watch the game with Uncle Jeff, right?"

Sam seemed to be contemplating the dilemma. "You bet football, watch Bruce and drink beer with Uncle Jeff," he said. "If he doesn't come out of the hospital, I can bet football and watch Bruce with you, but you'll have to find someone else to drink beer with."

The words seemed to leave his mouth in slow motion. As the meaning of Sam's innocent statement reached my brain, my heart threatened to collapse. "He's coming out of the hospital," I said.

"I know," Sam said.

I jumped off the couch and headed out of the room so that he didn't see the tears in my eyes. I cried all the way through the short drive to the hospital.

As usual, the waiting room was stuffed with members of the Fazzolari family. Lynn, Corinne, Chuck, Carrie, Mom, Dad and Jim and Lisa had spent nearly the entire day in the cramped, still-filthy room. Jeff had shared something with each one of them through the day. He'd said, 'Hi, Carrie' to his little sister, and 'Hey, buddy' to Dad. Yet soon after, he'd drifted off to sleep and was much less aware as the day progressed.

"He's not as awake as yesterday," John said. "Why is that?"

I shrugged. They were talking about slowing down the

drain on his brain a bit; perhaps the fact that he was doing more healing on his own caused him a bit of fatigue. "They say he's doing well," I said. "We have to trust the doctors."

"He's going to be pissed that he misses Bruce at halftime," John said. "I think there's at least twenty people taping it for him."

I had my own plan. I was going to see if I could wake him long enough so he could at least catch a glimpse of The Boss.

John handed me a cup of coffee. The game was just a few minutes from starting.

"Remember when we all saw Bruce at Darien Lake?" John asked.

"Yeah, that was a day," I said.

As the pre-game show wound down, I pressed my back against the hard red chair and got lost in the memory of the day gone by. Typically, Jeff had planned the particulars of the day's events and slowly drew me in to make the plan come together.

Outside of the usual holidays, there normally wasn't a more highly anticipated day of the year than any day Bruce Springsteen was in town. The talk of Bruce's Buffalo stop had sent us all scrambling in a lot of directions for the best possible seats. That year, Springsteen had originally booked Ralph Wilson Stadium for the show, but just a month before the concert was set to play, the venue changed to Darien Lake, the Six Flags Amusement Park some thirty minutes away. As soon as the change was announced, Jeff's telephone call rang through.

"We need to get a limo," he insisted.

"Dude, the tickets cost enough," I said. The idea of riding to the show in the height of luxury had never crossed my mind.

"Come on, call for the limo. It'll be perfect."

"Maybe if we all chip in," I said.

"We'll chip in," he said. "Think of how great it'll be."

Unbelievably, my wife thought it was a great idea. As usually happens with good ideas, the wives get together and take care of getting the job done. Kathy spoke with John and Dana, and soon enough the limo was in front of our house for the long, beer-filled ride to the park.

There are so many blocks of time in life that are lived and quickly forgotten. The evening spent with Springsteen was certainly most unforgettable.

Our tickets were spread all through the park. Jeff, with friends Brad Gier and Jeff Popple, were the furthest away from the stage, with John and Dana and Chris and Tina Miller settled in about halfway back in the crowded amphitheatre. Yet Kathy and I continued to walk closer and closer to the stage. Kathy had secured the tickets, paying premium price for the opportunity to get a closer look at Bruce and the band. Still, we were unprepared for the quality of the seat. We found ourselves just eight rows back, about thirty feet from where Bruce would be playing.

"Oh my God!" I said as we settled in. "It's too bad everyone else is back there."

Kathy didn't answer me, but I could tell that the wheels were turning. "Give me your ticket," she said.

"Why?" I asked, aggravated that I had to dig it out of my pocket.

"I'm going to get Jeff," she answered.

Springsteen had not even taken the stage yet, but I fiddled in my seat, believing that Kathy was going to be busted any minute and that we'd be escorted from the park. Moments later, I saw Jeff ambling toward me, holding the ticket high over his head.

"Evening Buffalo," Springsteen said as Jeff and Kathy settled into the space beside me. We had three people in two seats, but no one was sitting anyway, and no one noticed. The music began, Bruce's guitar pierced the air, and Kathy shouted out to Jeff, "You can stay for three songs and then I'll go and get John!"

"My dear sister-in-law, I'm not going anywhere," Jeff said as he hugged Kathy.

By the time the E Street Band ripped through the opening chords of Badlands, there were five of us standing in the spot that had been reserved for two. John, Dana, Kathy, Jeff and I squeezed into the tight area, our arms around one another, with each and every song serving as a loud reminder that we were in exactly the perfect spot.

Springsteen had played for nearly three hours by the time he ripped into the opening chords of Rosalita. I was happy enough with the choice of song, but even happier a minute later when Jeff ripped the baseball cap off my head and leaned down to kiss me, directly on the bald spot on the top of my head.

"This is unbelievable!" he screamed.

It was a nearly perfect day.

The television reception in the waiting room was horrendous. John, Jim and I kept one eye on the game as we took turns checking in on Jeff. The first quarter ended with the Steelers leading three to nothing, and I started laughing.

"What the hell are you laughing at?" John asked.

"Jeff and I just won $250," I said. "Those are our numbers in the pool."

"He's such a lucky bastard," Jim said. "Didn't you guys win money last year?"

"The year before," I said. "We won a grand on one of Jeff's squares. We always win on the one's he buys."

"Tell him," Jim said. "Maybe it'll wake him up in time to hear Bruce."

During the second quarter, John headed down the hall

to check in on his little brother. "He's asleep," he said as he stepped back into the waiting room. "He squeezed my hand when I first got in there, but now he's resting."

Even though the game was marked with fast-paced action, we were all having a hard time focusing on the drama. Bruce and the band were the real attraction of the game for us, and it was heartbreaking that Jeff would not join us for the performance. Yet I had to try.

I entered his room slowly. I grabbed his right hand and asked for a squeeze. I felt a slight squeeze back. "Hey, are you with me?" I asked.

Another squeeze!

"We won $250 on the first-quarter square," I said. Jeff battled to open his eyes. "We can use it to buy the meat." Jeff squeezed my hand harder.

"Say, Bruce is coming on in a few minutes. We're taping it for you to see later, but do you want to listen to it now?"

He raised those wonderful eyebrows as if to ask me what the hell kind of question that was. Of course he wanted to listen to Bruce!

I turned the television volume up as Bruce and the band took the stage.

"Tenth-Avenue Freeze-out," I announced as the familiar voice filled the room. "They look great," I said.

Jeff squeezed my hand. "Bruuuuce!" he whispered.

I barely heard the music over the sounds of my own breathing as I tried hard to stifle the sobs that were hammering away at my insides. Jeff should have been on his feet leading a great version of the song in his very own living room.

"Working on a Dream," I said as the band tore into their second song.

Yet this time there was no response from Jeff. I felt ridiculous for placing such importance on the performance.

It truly didn't matter if Bruce put on a good show or if he fell off the front of the stage. The next song was Born to Run, followed by Glory Days. Jeff hadn't opened his eyes or squeezed my hand in well over five minutes.

"Just rest," I whispered.

"Woo-hoo," Jeff croaked out at the perfect moment to match Bruce's vocal in Glory Days.

The sob that had been threatening me escaped into the air, but I swallowed real hard. "Our boy did good," I said.

"He did real good," Jeff whispered back, and for a split-second, we locked eyes.

We'd seen Bruce together over fifteen times. We'd cheered shoulder-to-shoulder in concert halls all over the country. We'd sung Thunder Road acapella on a porch in Fort Meyers, Florida, but we'd never had a more perfect Springsteen connection.

"I love you, brother," I whispered.

I have no way of knowing if he heard me.

Chapter VI – Living Proof

February 02 to February 05, 2009   When anxiety was great within me, your consolation brought joy to my soul.   PS 94:19

The drama of the Steelers last-minute Super Bowl victory was lost in the downward spiral of the day. Once the game ended, I knew that the waiting room would clear out and soon enough, it would just be the air mattress, the Pepsi machine and me. Yet Jim and Lisa took care of a couple of pressing items before they hit the road for the night. Jim pumped up the air mattress, and Lisa finally found someone from housekeeping who could vacuum the floor and empty the garbage cans.

By midnight everyone had returned home and I decided to check on Jeff once more before hitting the mattress. Peter was Jeff's nurse for the night, and it made me smile to hear Jeff whisper his question to me when I entered the room. "Can Peter Parker get me a drink?" he asked.

"He's calling you Peter Parker," I said.

"Yeah, he's been doing that all night," Peter said.

The television was on low, and I was surprised when Jeff turned his head to look at it just as the highlights of the game were played.

"Who won?" he asked.

"The Steelers," I said.

"Was it bad?" he asked.

"No, it was a close game. Arizona almost pulled it off."

Jeff nodded as though the end result met with his approval.

"We'll watch it together in a few days," I said. "We taped it for you."

Jeff's eyes closed slowly.

"We had to draw some blood," Peter said. "He had a little morphine a while ago, so he's probably going to be groggy for the night."

"Peter Parker," Jeff said, and both Peter and I laughed.

"He's a live wire, huh?" Peter asked.

"Oh, I could tell you some stories," I said.

I headed back to the waiting room with another story running through my mind.

As a family, we had made two separate trips to California and the towns where Dad was working as a construction project manager. In 1986, the family spent the summer in Mountain View, California, and every day Jeff, Jim and I played basketball on a full-length outdoor court.

The sound of Jeff alone on that court was enough to draw interest from anyone wanting to play a game. During those days he had reached his full height of six-foot three inches, but he was rail skinny and deceptively strong. He was also learning the game and the art of telling you how badly he was beating you.

During that wonderful summer in the San Jose area, the Fazzolari's were joined by lifelong fellow North Collins resident Scott Weiser, who was stationed just a few miles away, on the naval base in Mountain View. It was a tremendous coincidence that we learned of only because Dad had called Scott's father, Ward, just to shoot the breeze. Scott was a welcome adversary on the basketball court, at the dinner table and behind a few bottles of beer. He was right beside me as we attempted to harness the energy of Jeff during our daily pickup basketball games. Lifelong buddy Tom Rybak, a Shirley Road neighbor, also made the trip and provided great companionship on the West Coast.

Early one Sunday morning, Jeff shook me out of bed. "Come on, buddy, let's play a game before church. Pigs don't sleep as long as you."

I rolled over in bed and listened to the ball thwack-thwack-thwacking off the pavement outside the window. Reluctantly, I headed for the door, lacing my sneakers courtside as Jeff attempted to slam the ball, coming up just short of doing it.

"Game to twenty-one," he called out. "Basket out."

Jeff was chomping at the bit to finally take me down in a game of one-on-one. I realized that I was living on borrowed time and that sooner or later he would beat me, and that most likely I would never beat him again. After a few warm-up shots, I announced that I was ready.

The summer sun was beginning to climb and despite our early start, I was sweating profusely after just a few minutes of action. Guarding Jeff was difficult as he swung his elbows, reached over me with long, monkey-like arms and taunted me with each shot that swished through the net.

"It's twelve to ten, me," he said as he bounced the ball at the top of the circle. "We're going to have to write down the date because this is the morning when the baton is officially passed from you to me."

"Just play," I said.

Jeff broke hard to his left, but I matched his movements and we found ourselves just ten feet from the basket. He held his dribble, looked straight into my eyes, and brought his left arm up. I left my feet in an attempt to block the shot, but quickly realized that Jeff had changed directions. His quick pump-fake, the move that I had taught him, left me hanging in the air, scrambling to somehow still cover him. The end result of the play was the ball settling in the net just as my ankle made contact with the hard pavement.

"Thirteen to ten," Jeff announced.

I screamed in pain, rolling back and forth on the pavement. My entire immediate future was flashing before my eyes as I realized that I had shattered my ankle.

"Aw, come on, Nancy, don't be like that," Jeff said.

I was screaming. Tears filled my eyes as the pain raced from my already swollen ankle to my tattered brain.

"Are you quitting?" Jeff asked.

"Seriously," I cried out. "Go get some help!"

Jeff's expression changed. His smile faded as he considered that I was truly in pain. He quickly left the court, hustling back to the apartment. Moments later, he was back, kneeling beside me as I grew used to the overwhelming pain. He wrapped a towel with ice around my already swelling ankle and dabbed at the sweat on my forehead. As my breathing returned to normal his smile returned.

"You really shouldn't go for the pump fake when you're in the air," he said.

"I don't think I can stand up," I said. It was as if I could feel my heartbeat in my foot.

"Do you forfeit the rest of the game?" Jeff asked. He toweled more sweat off my brow.

"Yeah, you win," I said. "Now what am I going to do? I can't just lay here!"

"I thought of that too," Jeff said. He pulled a bottle of tanning lotion from his back pocket. "I brought you this. If you're going to lie on the pavement all day, I don't want you to burn."

We both laughed as the California sun beat down hard.

"What we've learned today is that I know how to pull off the pump fake, and you'll never beat me again," Jeff said.

Before too long, Jeff helped me up off the pavement. I wrapped my left arm around his shoulder and he helped me to the couch in the apartment. Despite the fact that my ankle healed nicely, Jeff had been right about the most important thing. I would never beat him again.

***

Back in the hospital waiting room I noticed that Jim had pumped up the mattress, but I couldn't get comfortable on it. Recounting the stories of Jeff's days was becoming tiresome. I no longer wanted the pain of remembering things. I wanted to get started on making new memories.

"Come on, God! Make him better!"

I started saying the rosary, but knew that I wouldn't make it past a couple of 'Hail Marys'. I thought of something a nun had told me back in my grammar school days. The angels will finish it for you if you start it and fall asleep.

The rosary fell from my hand as my eyes struggled closed. This one was on the angels.

I struggled off the mattress by 5:30a.m.and headed to the room. I couldn't believe that I'd slept for five hours straight. Peter was at the bedside, and Jeff was wide awake.

"We're taking him for an X-ray," Peter said. "He slept all the way through the night, but that's okay, rest is good."

I took Jeff's hand; he opened his eyes wide but didn't say anything.

"I can't believe I slept all the way through the night," I said. "I didn't even check on him once."

Peter's look was quizzical. "You were up," he said. "You came shuffling down the hall at about three, looked in at Jeff, made some sort of grunting sound and walked right back out. I have to tell you, we were laughing about it at the desk."

"Oh good, now I'm sleep-walking," I said.

"It's great, though," Peter said. "Your family being here around the clock is going to make a big difference to Jeff as he heals."

Jeff was wheeled from the room to X-ray at about six-thirty. When he returned by seven-fifteen, he was

surrounded by all of his brothers. Jim and John had ar-
rived during the time that Jeff was downstairs, and Jeff
acknowledged the gathering by winking at John as he re-
entered the room. John's eyes instantly filled with tears.

"It's good to see him awake," John said.

Peter took his time repositioning Jeff in bed. Jim edged
closer and looked down at Jeff smiling broadly as he did
so.

"Morning, sunshine," Jeff croaked out.

Moments later, Jeff was asleep once more.

On the way back to the waiting room, a sense of deep
frustration started to build in my mind. Thankfully Jim and
John were there to help me hold it at bay. "This is how
it's going to be for awhile," Jim said. "The injury he suf-
fered is horrible, but I know he'll be fine. He'll be as good
as new, you watch."

Jim handed me a cup of coffee. I saw that he'd also
brought a couple of dozen donuts for the nursing staff.
I gathered my clothes for the day and headed for the
men's room.

"Where are you going?" John asked.

"Believe it or not, I have to go to work today."

"Suck it up," John said. "I'm just coming off a 10-hour
shift."

Later in the day, for the first time since Jeff's stroke, I
was back on the road doing my job. I visited a few con-
struction sites, caught up on about a hundred e-mails and
worked on setting up a schedule so that I wouldn't wind
up in a hospital bed, too.

It felt strange to be out in the open air, worrying about
something as trivial as my job. Yet I'd been doing audits
of construction sites for nearly twenty years so I was on
automatic pilot that afternoon. My job consisted of watch-
ing others do their work, assessing their compliance with
OSHA regulations and writing detailed reports. The tele-

phone was never more than an inch away from my right hand, and midway through the day it rang. Despite the fact that I was driving I immediately answered it.

"What's up, Cliffy?" Carrie asked.

"Is everything okay?" I asked.

"Yeah, Jeff's doing fine," she said, "but I have to leave tomorrow, and it's killing me!"

The pain that Carrie was feeling wasn't lost on me. The minutes away from the hospital were difficult enough, but the prospect of having to leave the state during Jeff's recovery had to be overwhelming.

"I'll be back up here as soon as I can, but you guys are going to have to hold the fort for awhile." Carrie's voice cracked with emotion.

"It'll be all right," I said. "We have a pretty good schedule worked out. We'll be there for him."

"I know," Carrie cried. "It just sucks!"

That was the understatement of the year. I pulled the car to the side of the road. Traffic whizzed by me, but it was as though I were completely oblivious to every aspect of life other than what was happening to our family. I pounded my fist on the steering wheel as I cried. Over and over, I beat my open hands on the steering column, thinking of Carrie's pain, Corinne and Chuck's pain, John and Dana, Jim and Lisa's pain and Lynn's pain. When I thought of Mom and Dad I cried harder. And Kathy and my kids' pain! And Jeff and Lynn's children! Over and over, I pounded on the car as though it had caused the mess. The pain in my hands overtook the hurt in my heart, and I finally gave into common sense and stopped swinging my hands, but there was no way that I could control the tears. "It's not fucking fair!" I screamed.

Thankfully I was able to drive to the closest convenience store. The car stereo was playing a Tom Petty song that somehow caught my attention and forced me back into the real world once again. I struggled for air, wiped the tears away and looked at my red hands. "One day at a time," I whispered. "We can do this."

It took a while, but I finally composed myself enough to make it home in time for dinner. Kathy prepared steak and mashed potatoes, and the boys chattered endlessly about their school day. They didn't ask too many questions about Jeff's recovery, but they were relieved when I explained that in time he would be okay. As I helped Kathy clear the dinner dishes, she subtly brought up the subject of my appearance. "You look like hell."

"I'm all right," I said. I tried to stretch my face so that the bags under my eyes weren't quite so noticeable.

"I know you're going to do what you need to do," Kathy said, "but you have to think about coming home to sleep at night."

To be honest, after nearly a week on the air mattress, I had considered the possibility. "A couple more days," I said.

"All right," Kathy said. "But I'll go up there for a few hours now. You aren't allowed to do anything for the next few hours other than lie on the couch and watch television."

"I can do that," I said, and Kathy gave me a long hug that was sorely needed.

After another fitful night on the air mattress, I finally tossed it on top of the Pepsi machine and started my day. It was three-thirty in the morning. I sat in the hard brown chair, left the television silent, sipped on a coffee with a queen of hearts staring back at me and prayed. By five a.m. I headed to the window beside Jeff's bed, and the view captured my attention. I saw the City of Buffalo lit up before me, and it struck me that the sun would be rising soon and that so many people would just take it for granted.

"The sun rises, sets and rises again, and hardly anyone ever notices," I whispered to myself. "The rivers flow out to the sea, and the earth spins around, and we just don't notice. I'm noticing now, God. I'm noticing now."

Jeff stirred in the bed just as the thought raced across my brain. His eyes were wide open and he raised one eyebrow as if to call me close.

"Are you okay?" I asked.

"Phew," Jeff answered.

"What hurts?" I asked.

Jeff rolled his eyes and it was all I could do not to laugh. If he had the strength he would come back with a one-liner about how I could be so stupid to ask such a question. I wished I could take some of the pain, and I knew that there were enough people who loved him who would line up to take the rest.

"You're just having a timeout," I said. "You're going to be fine."

The expression on Jeff's face shifted to one of utter sadness, and I felt my heart tighten in my chest. "Have I ever steered you wrong?" I asked.

"Sometimes," Jeff whispered.

For a long moment we stared at one another. I tried hard to fix my face with a positive look, but Jeff's eyes were filled with sadness, love and resignation.

"You're trying too hard," I finally said. "You need to rest. Just close your eyes and rest. We're all right here."

By a quarter after seven the light of the rising sun had filled Jeff's room. The doctor spent a couple of moments at his bedside and then headed to the hall where Jim and I were stationed. We had learned early on that Jeff's doctor was a man of few words.

"His temp is a little high, but he's doing real well. He's moving forward. Jeff has a much better left hand grip. He's progressing."

"Is there a threat of pneumonia?" I asked.

"He's been in that bed for awhile now," the doctor responded. "If you or I were lying in one position, we'd be prone to developing pneumonia, but we're aware that it could happen, and we're on it. He's doing real well."

The doctor turned and headed down the hall. Jim smiled at me. "That's good," he said.

"It's not good enough," I answered.

Back at the bedside, the nurse for the day was laughing. I glanced at her name on the board beside the bed. I hadn't met Mary Lou before that morning. "Whose birthday is it?" she asked. "I wrote down the date and Jeff said, 'Happy birthday.'"

I looked over at Jim. For a moment we were both confused and were ready to write it off as some sort of hallucination. "Today is our niece Nicole's birthday," Jim said, remembering at last.

"Happy birthday," Jeff whispered.

My shift was officially over, as Jeff was in the capable hands of Jim. As I headed for the front door of the hospital, I thought of Jeff and how he'd remembered Nicole's birthday, and my mind shifted to the day of Nicole's baptism.

John and Dana chose Jeff to be Nicole's godfather, and once more he was determined to make the ceremony something that would never be forgotten. In an effort to keep everything straight for the ceremony, Dana made up cards that explained everyone's role in the event. Jeff's sign read, "I'm the godfather!"

In typical Jeff fashion, he changed the arrangement of the letters and wore his own version of the sign proudly; it proclaimed, "God I'm the father!"

It occurred to me that as much as I hated being at the hospital, I also despised being away, but, buoyed by the early morning activity, I headed back to work. Jim called to let me know that Jeff had tried to bribe the nurse for a tall glass of iced tea and that he'd asked who else was going to visit today. I called my mother and father to report the good news. Dad answered on the first ring, and the fatigue in his voice reminded me that there weren't very many people in our family who were resting well.

"Jeff's had a good morning," I said in an effort to eliminate any worry.

For the next twenty minutes we talked about the efforts of the hospital staff, the worries in our heart and the urgent need to stay strong.

"We're all going to get tired of this," I said, "and sooner or later we're going to start bitching at each other."

"I'm already tired of it," Dad said, "but we have to hang in there. We've been in tough places before, right?"

"Not this tough," I said.

"No, not this tough," Dad agreed.

As I hung up the telephone, I thought of Dad's own brush with mortality. In April of 1994, we all gathered at Millard Fillmore Hospital at Gates Circle in downtown Buffalo. Dad's kidney removal operation was underway. The doctors explained that it would be a lengthy ordeal, but that they were quite confident that the cancer was contained and that they'd be able to get it all.

Corinne was the leader of our group, and we were all taking our lead from our oldest sibling and the always-steady gaze of our brother-in-law Chuck. Corinne was in complete control of the situation, too, as she offered comfort to my mother, whose eyes betrayed the brave face that she was putting on for the touchy operation.

"He's going to be fine," Corinne continued to say reassuringly.

We were all so scared. Up to this point, cancer had never showed its face in the tight circle of our immediate family. We gathered in the cafeteria, sharing a light breakfast and a few cups of coffee. I scanned the faces of my siblings. John, who was always the strongest, looked as if he were about to absolutely break down and start to blubber. Dana was beside him as usual.

Jim, who had earned the nickname as my father's pet by following Dad from room to room, was absolutely beside himself with grief and worry. He was saying little more than please and thank-you. Carrie actually was crying a little bit, and Corinne was trying her best to make her little sister laugh.

Jeff and I were seated together in a quiet corner of the cafeteria. Mom and Corinne had headed outside for a cigarette to calm their nerves. John and Jim took to pacing the halls outside the waiting room.

For what seemed like the first time in his life, Jeff wasn't talking much.

I allowed the silence to take control. I was having a difficult time pondering why my father was so sick. My mind was playing tricks on me because for all of my life, my father had seemed absolutely invincible. How could he be in so much trouble now?

"It's amazing," Jeff said to break the silence.

"What's amazing?" I asked.

"The life that Mom and Dad have lived."

I knew exactly what he meant. My mother and father were true heroes to all of us.

"Think of all that they've accomplished together," Jeff said. "Through thick and thin, in sickness and in health, they have just brought so much love. If I can bring half as much love into the world, I will have been a successful man."

I wasn't used to Jeff digging so deep to express his feelings.

"Dad's going to be all right, isn't he?" Jeff asked.

When he looked into my eyes, I saw that my answer

would have a lot of impact. If I reflected his worry back at him, he would break down in tears. If I showed a brave face of defiance, he would adopt the same stance.

"Of course he'll be fine," I said as my own voice broke. "God rewards faith. Let's just be strong for Mom."

Hours later Jeff and I stood shoulder-to-shoulder at the foot of my father's bed. The operation had been considered a success. The cancer had been contained and Dad was on the road to recovery. We shared a hug in the waiting room and as Jeff and I returned to our cars in the parking lot, he repeated the words to our little conversation in the waiting room.

"If I can bring half as much love into the world I will have been successful," he said.

"Amen," I said. "Get some rest, dude. You'll be successful beyond your wildest dreams."

Jeff laughed and flipped me the bird. "See you here tomorrow."

***

As Jeff struggled in his own battle for health, we were all quite aware that as the week progressed, the sense of frustration would grow, and that slowly but surely, we would tire of one another and our trips back and forth to the hospital. Of course, there weren't any outward signs of the struggle, as everyone tried hard to make do, but sleep deprivation was taking its toll. I had a growing sense that something was going wrong in Jeff's care, but the information was slow in coming.

The first order of business was to be a minor operation that would move the feeding tube from the center of Jeff's nose to his stomach. The staff seemed a little concerned with the fact that Jeff had not regained the ability to swallow, and the threat of pneumonia and the build-up of saliva were two more major concerns. In the middle of it all, not quite understanding all that needed to happen, I felt myself sliding away. Why couldn't he just get better? When would he sit up in bed and offer me a sarcastic smile that told me that he'd just been kidding, and that it had been his all-time number one practical joke?

On Thursday evening, Corinne and I informed the staff that there would not be anyone sleeping on the floor of the waiting room. True to her nature, Corinne organized the effort by printing up cards that held all of our telephone numbers in case of an emergency. Still, as we sat in the waiting room, discussing the next day's schedule, a cloud of frustration hung in the area, threatening to smother us.

"I feel bad," I said, "but I've hardly had the chance to talk to either Lynn or Mom and Dad. They've been coming in during the afternoon, and I haven't even seen them."

"Yeah, well, we all have a little piece of it," Corinne said. "We need to just continue on and remember that we're all pulling on the same end of the rope. We'll stay here for two years if we have to, right?"

Maybe, but we could not stay any longer that night. I was scheduled for a long trip to Syracuse for work the next day, and Corinne was also due to punch in early. We stood up at the same time and headed for the elevators.

"You know what absolutely killed me today?" Corinne asked.

"Oh please tell me a sad story," I said.

"I was in Jeff's room, and he was sort of looking out the window. I was whispering to him, and he just wailed, 'Johnny, Johnny, Johnny!'"

"Oh God," I said.

"And he got this longing look on his face. I just blubbered right in front of him."

"How could you not?" I asked.

The elevator made its descent as Corinne and I shared

a cry in the sinking car. On the way through the parking ramp, memories of Johnny's birth year flooded my brain.
***

It was the summer of 2001 and life was wonderful. There were children running around the home on Shirley Road for each and every event, and pride was shining in the eyes of John and Lynda who had envisioned such a life when they had started their own family all of those years ago.

Jeff and Lynn were anxiously awaiting their addition to the party. Lynn's pregnancy was developing nicely, and names were being bantered about as the child was expected in late December. Yet life changed quite a bit for every American on a clear September morning.

Jeff was as upset about what happened on 9/11 as anyone, but his frustration was also centered on the reactions of those around him as he continued to work on that fateful day.

"I was trying to prepare a dinner for about five-hundred people when the planes hit," he said. "Of course we all watched in horror, but word quickly came down that the event was still a go, so we had a lot of work to be done in a short window of time. The problem was I couldn't get anyone to do his or her job. There was one guy, who was about five-feet-five and three hundred pounds, walking around the dining hall, smashing his fist into his hand. After watching him carry on for over an hour, I finally went to him. He asked me if I'd seen what happened, and I told him that it was our job to keep moving forward. The guy was just beside himself so I finally asked him what he wanted to do about it."

"I'm going to go fight," the man responded.

"You're going to fight?" Jeff asked. "You can't even cut up the lettuce."

The rest of Jeff's crew had received the message.

The event went off as planned, and life moved forward. Things were certainly different, and many tears were cried, but perhaps the best of all lessons learned was that we had to work together to get through the pain.

The horrific fall was followed by a truly wonderful holiday season. Without question the most wonderful news of all arrived on the morning of December 17, 2001.

"I have my living proof," Jeff said.

"What happened?" I asked. I knew that he was calling from the hospital.

"Lynn had the baby at three-twenty-three. He's seven pounds and two ounces and twenty-one inches long. He's perfectly healthy. He's absolutely beautiful."

Jeff's voice was different somehow. Having been present at the birth of my own children, I knew that he was at the very pinnacle of life. I appreciated that he was as happy as he'd ever be.

"What're you going to name him?" I asked.

Jeff paused for a long moment as if he were possibly stifling a tear and sure enough, his voice came back to me, broken up. "Johnny," he said. "After Dad. I had to name him after Dad."

"I can't imagine a better Christmas for any of us," I said. "I'm proud of you, and so proud of Lynn. That's awesome."

Jeff had a number of telephone calls yet to make, but before he let me go, there was one more thing that he wanted to say.

"Dude," he said, "If there was ever a man who witnessed the birth of his child, and didn't come away believing in God, then he's a real idiot."

"Living proof," I said. "Living proof."

Chapter VII – All that Heaven Will Allow

February 06 to February 11, 2009   I've learned that people will forget what you said, people will forget what you did, but people will never forget how you made them feel.
Maya Angelou

I didn't want to do it, but it had to be done. As I headed back to Buffalo from my daylong stint in Syracuse, I took a deep breath, slipped the Springsteen CD into the slot and tortured myself with the songs from the Working on a Dream disc. Springsteen's voice filled the car, and I couldn't stop the tears from falling. I concentrated on Thanksgiving Day in 2008 and the questions of life and death that had plagued Jeff just hours after we'd finished off the turkey at Mom and Dad's.

The pain in Jeff's back was creating real havoc, but his November had also been shattered by the loss of a close friend, Matt Roe, who had been killed in an industrial accident. The sudden loss of his former co-worker left Jeff searching for answers, and to all of his siblings Jeff's pain was front and center.

After the Thanksgiving meal at Mom and Dad's, Jeff and I had a long conversation as I drove with him back to his home. The drive started innocently enough as he blasted his all-time favorite song, American Land by Springsteen.

"Turn it down!" I shouted.

"Let's stop for a beer," Jeff said.

"It's Thanksgiving night," I said. "There isn't even a bar open."

Jeff leaned back in the seat. Bruce's voice filled the truck at the highest of all possible settings. I finally reached across and lowered the volume.

"I'm going to tickle you," Jeff said.

"No you're not," I said, laughing. "I'm driving."

"I might tickle you," he said.

I turned my gaze from the road for a moment, just long enough to catch his smile.

"I'm kind of reeling," he said as he lowered the volume on the radio even more.

I was well aware of where the conversation was headed. I knew that Jeff was thinking about his friend, Matt, as well as the devastation caused with his passing. Matt's wife, Andrea, would be forced to raise two children alone.

"It just hurts me to think of that young family being torn apart," he said. "Matt was a good man, and just like that, it's over."

"Yeah, that's horrible," I said.

"Don't you worry about that?" Jeff asked. "What would your family do without you?"

"I try hard not to think about it," I said. "That's why I take such good care of myself."

Both Jeff and I laughed. He leaned across the seat and tickled me before I had the chance to slap his hand away. I jerked the wheel a bit, but he stopped tickling me and slipped back against the seat, cranking the sound up on American Land. For good measure, he started the song over again and leaned back in the seat to sing the first verse. When the verse was over, he lowered the volume once more.

"We'll make a deal," he said. "If anything ever happens, we take care of each other's family."

"I don't even think we need to mention it," I said.

"I know," he said.

***

Just two and half months later, on that Saturday morning in early February, the hospital waiting room was filled with family and friends, including Tom and Cherrie Rybak and my college buddy Terry Hancock who had made the trip from Rochester. The Gow School where Jeff worked as executive chef was also well represented; Headmaster Brad Rogers stopped in, along with Jeff's good friend Paul Rose, who visited with his wife and children. Yet the nightmare was just continuing. Jeff spent the entire day fairly non-responsive, sleeping his way through the morning and early afternoon. Yet before I headed back to my family for the day, leaving Jeff's care in the capable hands of Corinne and Chuck, I ducked my head into Jeff's room. Of course, his eyes were shut.

"Dude," I whispered. "Give me something today, huh?"

I took Jeff's hand and offered a slight squeeze. I felt a faint pressure.

"So, you hear me, huh? I was listening to Springsteen yesterday. He said 'Hi' by the way."

I felt a stronger squeeze, and it brought a smile to my lips.

"Remember when we were in Florida and we sang Thunder Road on the porch overlooking the water?"

This time there wasn't a response. The now-familiar wave of frustration swept over me once more.

"Come on, one time," I whispered. "The screen door slams, Mary's dress waves. Like a vision she dances across the porch as the radio plays."

I couldn't stop the tears from falling. Jeff offered another weak squeeze, so I sang the line again. As the words radio plays left my mouth, I heard a whisper. Now, someone else might think I had imagined it, but I heard it as clear as a tolling bell.

"Roy Orbison singing for the lonely," Jeff whispered.

I had exactly what I needed for the day.

On Sunday morning I arrived at the hospital a little after six to find Jim sitting in the waiting room, sipping coffee with our buddy Jeff Popple.

"Good afternoon," Jim said. He handed me a coffee.

"How long have you guys been here?" I asked.

"Too long," Pops said.

"Yeah, really," I said. I grabbed the coffee and plopped down on the hard brown plastic chair next to Pops.

"You know what we're amusing ourselves with today?" Pops asked.

"What's that?" I asked.

"Our vacation when we saw the Yankees play the Orioles. Remember that one?"

Pops laughed. "Jeff was in rare form."

"He sure was," I agreed.

It didn't take much coaxing from Jim to tell the entire story.

For months, Jeff and I worked hard to plan our vacation. Our original plan was to drive to Fenway Park to watch the Red Sox battle the Yankees and then drive down the Atlantic coast to see the Yankees face the Baltimore Orioles. Day after day we talked it out. We made the necessary travel arrangements, took the time off of work and talked Jeff Popple into joining us for the trip. At the very last minute we cancelled the trip to Boston, deciding instead to just spend the entire week in Baltimore where we could meet up with our good friends Jeff Taylor (Fluffy) and Mike Palmer (Rosie).

The drive to Baltimore was an adventure in itself, as we had decided to travel at night in an effort to beat the traffic and handle the four hundred miles in record time. About one hundred miles into the trip, Jeff, already tiring, turned to me. "Do you feel like driving some?"

I've always had a hard time driving in the dark. Driving in the rain isn't my favorite thing either. Unfortunately, it was the dead of night and we were caught in a torrential downpour. "I'm not real comfortable with it," I said.

After a bit of coaxing, Jeff switched places with Pops, who had been fast asleep in the backseat. "Just let me rest for about an hour and I'll take the wheel again," Jeff said.

Fifteen minutes later, we were checking into a hotel nearly five hours away from our final destination. Pops had been unable to keep the car on the road, hitting the rumble strips as he teetered on the edge of sleep and coherency. It wasn't to be the last hiccup on the trip.

Jeff Taylor and Mike Palmer are close friends from my days at college, and they were certainly looking forward to our arrival. Yet both men were still at work when we finally arrived in Baltimore in the late morning. We were forced to wait for them outside of their locked apartment doors. The summer temperature was approaching a hundred degrees.

"What the hell are we going to do all afternoon?" Jeff asked.

"We can just sit here and wait," I said.

Pops seemed content to take my recommendation.

"We're going to waste a perfectly good day?" Jeff asked.

"What do you suggest?" I asked.

"Follow me," Jeff said.

Moments later we were in the car, driving through the unfamiliar streets, just looking for something that caught Jeff's eye. I was more than a bit apprehensive, but soon enough we found an arcade and batting cage. For the next two hours, we swung at ninety mph pitches and played countless games of air hockey and video golf. I could almost tell what was coming next.

"I'm parched," Jeff said.

Half an hour later we were driving through the streets of Baltimore with a case of beer icing in a small cooler.

"We need to find a place to drink those," Jeff said.

"We'll just go back to Fluffy's apartment and sit on the sidewalk," I suggested.

Jeff glanced into the backseat, shrugged his shoulders and said, "That's what I'd expect you to say. You always have to be careful, right? What do you think, Pops? If you had one wish, what would you like to do right now?"

"I'd like to do a cannonball into an in-ground swimming pool," Pops said.

"That's exactly what we're going to do!" Jeff said excitedly.

"What is this, Ferris Bueller's Day Off?" I asked.

"Don't you worry your pretty head about it," Jeff said. "My buddy Pops wants to swim, so we're going to swim."

Ten minutes later Pops and I followed Jeff through the lobby of the downtown Holiday Inn. Rather than trying to sneak into the hotel unnoticed, Jeff walked straight to the front desk, holding the cooler of beer.

"Which way to the pool?" he asked the girl behind the counter. She hesitated ever so slightly and Jeff leaned in to read her nametag. "My God, Julie, you're a good-looking girl. Is your shift almost over?"

Julie's face went a couple of shades of red. She smiled as I clutched Pops' arm and watched the rest of the show.

"We have ice-cold beers in here and we'd certainly appreciate it if you'd join us. Wouldn't we, boys?"

"This isn't going to work," I whispered to Pops.

"Yeah, it will," he whispered back. "I'll give you ten to one odds that she drinks a beer with us."

Ten minutes later we were in the pool. Julie joined us when her shift was over. She drank two beers and laughed harder than she'd ever laughed in her life. I guarantee it. And our vacation was just getting started.

For the next five days, we spent time with our friends. We attended three straight Yankee-Orioles games that all had the same outcome: the Yankees won big. Dressed in our Yankee garb, we were true nuisances to our Baltimore hosts, but the trip couldn't have been any more successful.

We spent a day visiting Aunt Carolyn and Uncle Lenny. We shared expertly made pasta, and laughed with our cousins until our faces were numb.

We played in a golf tournament during a torrential downpour that chased everyone off the course except our foursome, with Jeff leading the way.

"It's only water," he maintained.

"Unless we get blasted by lightning," Pops cautioned.

"Always the pessimist," Jeff said. "Keep golfing."

The only downside of the trip was that we eventually had to make the long trip home. Unfortunately, the journey began with an epic traffic jam on a 95-degree day on the Maryland highway. The air conditioning in Jeff's Cougar wasn't working properly, so we were baking in the sun as not a single car moved for nearly an hour.

"This blows," Jeff said. Sweat was racing down his face.

"I'm thirsty," Pops said from the backseat.

"You think?" Jeff asked. "Why don't you pass me an ice-cold bottle of water?"

"From where?" Pops asked. He was growing excited. "Where is it?"

"We don't have any," Jeff answered and laughed. All at once, I saw the wheels turning in my little brother's mind. "But that doesn't mean we can't get some," he said. He turned to look at me. "If traffic starts moving, pull the car up a little. You can handle that, can't you? Don't smash into the car in front of you."

"Where are you going?" I asked. "Come on, don't be stupid. What if traffic starts moving?"

He was already out of the car.

"I swear to God it's like taking a nine-year-old girl on a trip. Relax," Jeff said. He leaned into the open window and winked at Pops. "Trust me."

"Baaaaah!" Pops said from the back of the car. He too had grown used to Jeff's impulsive ways.

For the next ten minutes we sat in traffic, not moving, but scanning all areas for any signs of Jeff.

"Do you have bail money for him?" Pops asked at one point.

I was getting nervous. I wasn't sure what sort of trouble he could get into, but I knew well enough that something was about to happen.

All at once, the traffic began to move. I shifted into the driver's seat and pulled the car ahead about a tenth of a mile. I was simmering in the heat. We were in the center lane with little chance to get over and wait for our wandering spirit.

"If we have to take off, I'm leaving him. I swear to God, I'll let him hitchhike home."

The words were no sooner out of my mouth than the passenger side door opened and Jeff leaped in.

"I heard that," he said. "And for being so doubting, you don't get an ice-cold water."

He tossed a bottle of water and a small purple Huggy drink to Pops in the backseat. He held at least four more drinks in his lap.

"Did you go to a store?" I asked.

Jeff made an exaggerated gulping sound as he sipped the water, taunting me with each swallow. "God, it's cold," he said.

The cars began moving ahead. The cotton in my mouth was threatening to make my head explode, but I wasn't going to give him the satisfaction by begging for the water. After a few eternally long minutes, he uncapped a bottle for me.

"I went for a walk," he said. "Finally I spotted what I was looking for, a fully stocked RV. The people couldn't have been any nicer. I told them that I had two kids who were suffering from dehydration and they set me up. I tried to get them to kick over some beer, but they asked why I'd give beer to children, so I just took the water."

"Unbelievable!" Pops called out.

"Problem solved," Jeff said. "And now you get to drive for awhile."

Yet the drive was eventful for one other reason. As we closed in on New York state, we tuned the radio to hear the details of O.J. Simpson's infamous slow ride down the California highway with the entire world watching.

O.J. had been our childhood idol as he ran through defenses as a Buffalo Bill. We listened, horrified, as we considered that he might actually shoot himself. Imagining the scene as it was described on the radio was an experience that could only be classified as weird.

"It's horrible," I said. "He had the whole world in the palm of his hand and now he's about to kill himself."

Jeff shrugged. "Sometimes people get lost," he said. "It doesn't matter how much money you have, either. If you get lost, you stay lost. There isn't anybody who can save you. But that's why the only heroes I have are the people I know."

It was actually quite a profound statement for a man who had scammed drinks from a family in an RV, but he was right. Still, I waited for the punchline.

"You're my hero," he said as he reached across the seat and tried to tickle me.

I jumped out of the way. "Knock it off, would you?"

Back at the hospital, Monday arrived and the thought of beginning another long week of healing was daunting, but everyone was digging even deeper. There had been plenty of signs that told us that Jeff would beat back the illness, but that it would be the longest of roads. My schedule for the day included another fairly long road trip, as I was teaching a class in Geneva about 120 miles away from the hospital. Thankfully, Jim and John planned to spend the entire day by Jeff's side. Lynn, Mom and Dad were also spending hour after hour with Jeff, so I surrendered a bit of control. Corinne, Chuck and Kathy would handle the late afternoon and the early evening hours.

Despite the fact that I had I returned to my bed at home, I wasn't sleeping much better. There were hours when sleep was heavy and refreshing, but there was the dreaded moment when my eyes cracked open and the grim reality hit me like a hurricane.

On Monday morning, I struggled out of bed with the words to an Our Father already on my lips. "Let Jeff have a great day, please!" I begged.

I dressed quickly and backed the car out of the driveway before the windows had even fully defrosted. It was ten minutes after five, and I'd left the house without waking Kathy or the boys, but as I drove I wondered if I were awake either!

The parking ramp was deserted at that time of day, and I drove to the upper floor where I'd be able to take the covered tunnel to the hospital door. My plan was to grab a couple of cups of coffee in the cafeteria before heading to Jeff's room. In my mind's eye, I could see him sitting up in bed, saying, "Good morning, pumpkin."

The cafeteria lights were dimmed, but the vending machine was open for business. I fished in my pocket for the correct change and automatically punched the number. The coffee cup dropped and I looked at the nine of spades. The second cup was being filled when I heard voices behind me. I turned quickly and saw the same doctor who'd checked Jeff into the hospital on the first night. We locked eyes, and I tried hard to search my memory banks for his name, but all I managed was a hurried, "Good morning."

The doctor's eyes flashed a look of recognition, and I wondered if he remembered telling us that Jeff would need a miracle to ever play basketball again. On this morning those same eyes looked straight through me, and I registered one more thought in the split-second of our crossing paths. "I don't have time to talk to you right now," he said. "I'm working with another patient, and I can't answer your questions."

He made a dismissive motion with his hand as he turned back to the other doctor walking with him.

"All I fucking said was 'Good Morning,'" I responded. I wanted to grab the man by the front of his shirt and explain to him that the fact that he had other things on his mind didn't concern me. He wasn't that busy, was he? I had a momentary flash of a dream in which I smashed him against the coffee machine until he crumpled to the floor. Instead I grabbed the second cup of coffee and turned away.

"Oh! I'm sorry, good morning," he said to my back.

I returned his dismissive wave to him. I was in no mood for any of this. Fuck him.

I entered Jeff's room slowly. He was sleeping peacefully and breathing evenly. I should have been happy that he appeared to be resting comfortably, but I had talked myself into the idea that he'd be sitting up waiting for me. I pulled the chair close to the bed and sipped the coffee, just waiting and praying, praying and waiting. Absolutely nothing happened over the next hour, but as I sat there watching my brother sleep I thought of long-forgotten days. Like my other siblings I'd shared so much with my brother, and no one could ever take that from any of us, but it still hurt to consider that instead of laughing and sharing I was waiting and praying. As Jeff slept, my mind went way back to a time when we were all children who dreamed of being best friends forever.

***

The early 1970s were a confusing time for most Americans. The unemployment rates were high. The Viet Nam war was stumbling to a chaotic conclusion. Richard Nixon was in charge and following his lead was difficult, or so I'm told. I was just a nine-year-old boy, trying to find something fun to do. It was a good thing that I had a number of playmates sharing the same home as me. Yet for a brief time that home was not the beautiful new place in North Collins, New York. Instead, in March 1974, the family was relocated to Largo, Florida, so that Dad could complete a large construction project.

Our temporary home was a beautiful place tucked in on a quiet street. There was a huge pond in the back-yard, with a deck where my brothers and I could cast our lines and pull out as many fish as we cared to catch. The family albums contain photos of four brothers and two sisters, tan, smiling and gathered by the water. Each boy looks exactly the same, brown skin, shaved head, shorts and the smile. Those days seemed to pass quickly, but the memories will never fade.

Early in the day on April 4th, 1974, my father gathered gear for a crab-catching expedition. We had small alu-minum basket-type nets that were lowered to the water with a raw chicken leg tied securely to each basket. The plan was to lower the nets, wait a little while and then pull them up. With any luck, the baskets would be filled with crabs gathered around the chicken leg.

Keeping an eye on four boys around a body of water is not an easy task, so my father did what he could. He went to the bridge to lower the traps with John and Jim. He asked me to stay on the shore with Jeff, who at nearly four years of age was ready to follow Dad into the water. For good measure, Dad allowed us to keep an eye on the twelve pieces of Kentucky Fried Chicken that he brought for our lunch.

Jeff and I waited on the shore. The trip to the bridge seemed to be taking way too long, so I handed Jeff a chicken leg and headed to where John, Jim and my father were gathered. Thinking back, it was awfully irresponsible to leave him alone, but he seemed content to eat and wait.

On the bridge, John and Jim raised the baskets. The idea was to greet the crabs by clicking off their claws so that they couldn't snap us. Then we would toss them into a huge bucket to take home and eat. Jim raised the net, John reached in and the first crab grabbed hold of John's right hand. I heard John's scream of pain and he crashed the pliers down hard on the shell of the crab, obliterating it.

"That's not what I had in mind," my father said. Then he turned to me. "Where's Jeff?"

"He's on the shore eating the Kentucky Fried Chicken," I said.

"Go back and watch him," my father said.

I headed back to the shore. Jeff was laying flat on his back. There were bones of six pieces of chicken beside him. He was holding another chicken leg, raising it to his mouth every few moments.

"What're you doing?" I asked.

"Eating the chicken," he said.

"You weren't supposed to eat it all," I said.

"You shouldn't have left it in front of me then," Jeff said.

Later that night, we all gathered around the television set. The Atlanta Braves were facing the Los Angeles Dodgers. Dad placed us all in front of the television set so that we could watch history being made. Henry Aaron had tied Babe Ruth as the homerun king with 714. Aaron walked his first time up and we all grew a little restless.

"Keep watching," Dad said.

John's hand was bandaged from his run-in with the crab. Jim was a little distracted, wondering why a baseball game being played by others was such a big deal. Jeff, with a belly full of chicken, was seated beside John, twirling John's hair in his fingers. I was as close to the television as I could be, rooting on Hammering Hank. Dad was making sure that none of us missed the moment.

Aaron strolled to the plate as Dad reminded us that Al Downing was a pitcher who had once toiled for our beloved Yankees. The announcers were speaking of the hate mail that Aaron had received as he threatened the record held by Babe Ruth.

"Why do they hate him?" I remember asking my father.

"Because he's black."

I didn't have time to process all that it meant. Aaron drove the ball deep to left center field. It cleared the wall, and we all cried out. I remember the moment clearly, and not just because it was a historic moment in the life of Henry Aaron. When that ball cleared the wall, the love of baseball was clearly defined in the lives of four boys and their father.

"That was great!" I told my dad.

Years later the images of that day remain clear in my mind's eye. There was Aaron's trip around the bases, the crab clinging to John's hand, Jeff twirling John's hair while sucking his own thumb and Jeff flat on his back on the beach with a huge belly full of at least seven pieces of chicken. Lessons learned: the Fazzolari boys would always love baseball, and more importantly, we would eat everything placed in front of us.

The colorful memories continued to play in my mind

through the rest of the morning. I handed off Jeff's care and drove the one hundred twenty miles to an OSHA safety training class in Geneva, New York. It felt ridiculous to stand in front of sixty people teaching, but I had to continue to stumble forward no matter what was happening in Jeff's hospital room.

As I spoke of fall protection, I was caught mid-sentence as my cell phone vibrated in my pocket. The call screen said, 'Jim.'

"Everyone take a break," I said.

There was a slight moan from the gathering, but the company representative, Robert Lamb, knew what I was up against.

"Take as much time as you need," he said as I began talking to Jim.

"What's up?" I asked him.

"Pal, they have to put him back on the ventilator," Jim said. "He's been sleeping so much that they're worried that he'll just get so comfortable that he won't come out of it."

From the top of my head to the tip of my toes it felt as though I were on fire. I could feel Robert's eyes on me.

"Should I come home?" I asked Jim.

"What're you going to do?" Jim asked. "We're here, and he's stable. Lynn is in with him now and so are Mom and Dad."

I couldn't find the right words to respond.

"You still there?" Jim asked.

"I'm here," I said.

The conversation was going to stumble to a conclusion somehow, but neither Jim nor I could push it ahead.

"I'll keep you posted," Jim said. "It's a good thing," he added. "They're on top of the care."

"I suppose," I whispered.

Yet how could it be good news? The tubes and wires

were supposed to be coming off, not going back in.

"Are you okay?" Robert asked. "You can head out if you need to."

"No, let's do it," I said. "The show must go on."

The class was ushered back in. I took a huge gulp of air and started the training once more. I told a long joke that brought hearty laughter from the men and women before me, but I felt absolutely ridiculous doing so. As I taught, I thought of Jeff and the grace and laughter that he brought to every single day.

"Keep 'em laughing," he would've been whispering in my ear.

As I drove back toward the hospital I considered what Jeff had tried to tell me two days before the stroke: try to enjoy life instead of trying to understand it. I cried as I considered how he spent each and every day trying to make others laugh. My younger brother had always looked up to me, but as I covered mile after lonely mile I realized that I admired him just as much because it wasn't just the main events that Jeff got primed for; everyday living and his ability to shock people gained him the most laughs. There are people who suffer through day after day, believing that their lives can never get better. Jeff was put on the earth to show them that it could.

Every event was the chance to get together, play hard and force the other guy to drink beer that he didn't truly want to drink. One day Jeff made the telephone calls to set up a basketball shooting match in the backyard. Life-long friends Jeff Popple and Chris Heinold were planning to meet Jim, John, Jeff and me for the shoot-around. The afternoon seemed likely to be a lasting memory.

Before our guests were to arrive, Jeff and I headed to the grocery store to get the necessary beer. I nestled in the passenger seat, listening to Bob Seger at full volume. Jeff had already decided on the teams and the drinking rules. At the store, he moved through the aisles, saying hello to everyone he knew. In our small town, going to the grocery store was a social event. We knew everyone, and everyone was aware of our business. We filled the cart with beer and headed for the checkout line. The cashier, Betty, a friend of my mother, was certainly aware that we were both old enough to purchase the beer. Yet it was her job to ask us for identification. "Do you have proof of birth?" she asked.

Jeff looked at me and I recognized the sly grin taking control of his face. He raised his eyebrow in my direction, and then turned to the past-retirement-aged woman. Slowly he raised his t-shirt to reveal his navel.

"I have a belly button. That's proof of birth, isn't it?"

Betty laughed, as did everyone within earshot.

"Jeffrey, you know I need to see a picture," she said.

"Come on," Jeff said. "You know how old I am."

He made a grand gesture of digging through his wallet. He took out a prayer card with a photo of Baby Jesus in the arms of Joseph.

"Here's a shot of me and my Dad when I was a baby," he said.

Betty examined the photo and laughed once more. Finally, Jeff slid his driver's license across the conveyor belt.

Satisfied that Jeff was indeed over twenty-one, she rang up the beer, and announced the total. Jeff handed her a fifty-dollar bill.

"Ah, my change drawer is low," Betty said. "Do you have anything smaller?"

Jeff took the bill back. In a grand gesture, he removed a twenty from his wallet and held it up with the fifty. He glanced at me, raising his eyebrows one more time.

"Seems to me they're all the same size," he said to Betty.

Once more everyone within earshot laughed. Keith Nelligan, another longtime family friend and a former store manager who just happened to be in the store, finally called out, "Come on, Fuzzy. Stop torturing Betty."

As we loaded the beer into the cart, Betty turned to me. "How do you put up with him?"

"Every day is a holiday and every meal is a feast," I said.

Jeff leaned over the counter and hugged Betty good-bye. As we walked out of the store, he shook every hand and joked with every man, woman and child who dared to acknowledge him.

Back in the car, he cranked up the stereo once more. I turned down the volume for a second. "You're exhausting," I said.

"Let's go, boy!" he sang out.

Seconds later we were back on the road, with Night Moves blaring out of the speakers and Jeff singing the words at the top of his lungs.

To him, it was just another day. Just twenty-four more hours to make everyone around him smile.

The memories of days gone by hammered my tired brain as I covered the ground from Geneva to Buffalo in record time, going directly to the hospital. Nearly every member of my family and our friends Larry Bowman, Chris Miller, Chris and Andrea Heinold with their daughters Taylor and Jordan, were standing in the hallway, just as we'd done on the very first evening.

"He's okay," Andrea said to me as I stepped off the elevator and into her strong hug. "It's all part of the healing process."

"Why is he sleeping so much?" I asked. I looked to Jim for some sort of answer. His eyes were drooping, and it dawned on me that he'd been on the floor since before the sun rose.

"They say it's from increased levels of fluid on the brain. Hopefully he'll start to come around again before too long."

During the course of the day the story broke that Alex Rodriguez of the Yankees had taken steroids. In an effort to break up the tension, Chris Heinold broached the subject. "What do you think of A-Rod?" he asked.

"I couldn't give two shits about A-Rod," I answered.

"Yeah, me neither," Chris said. "We just have to get the boy feeling better."

Within an hour the hallway cleared out, leaving me alone again with my thoughts. I called Kathy to explain that I'd be home soon, but she was on top of things at home and told me not to rush.

The visit to Jeff's bedside brought absolute anguish as I considered the ventilator and the fact that we wouldn't be hearing his voice anytime soon. The idea that the humming ventilator was necessary for Jeff to stay alive was disgusting to me. I hated the ventilator and every tube that was attached to his body. Jeff wasn't supposed to be in such a position. He was supposed to be setting up the next basketball shoot-a-round.

"Please, God, please!" I cried in the silence of the room.

I edged away from the bed and my eyes made contact with a prayer that Lynn had posted on the corkboard in the center of the room. I said the prayer over and over again, hoping that it would help somehow. One thing was sure, though, it was not easing my tears. How was I supposed to be offering worship? Didn't God have a hand in everything that was happening? Couldn't he have stopped this somehow? 'Worship' and 'adoration' weren't words at the forefront of my mind. Jeff didn't deserve this. Lynn and the kids didn't need to go through this. What sort of loving God would put a healthy man in such a position?

I headed back to the empty waiting room, feeling as though my presence was absolutely useless to the process. If God were listening, there had to be a plan of sorts, didn't there? I listened to a couple of nurses chattering as they walked down the hall. They were speaking of one of the reality shows that they'd watched the other night. I had a reality show for them, and it wasn't very entertaining. Much as I felt when confronting the doctor in the morning I wanted to grab hold of them and tell them to get their priorities straight. "Worry about your patients," I muttered to myself.

All at once, a sound blared through the speakers overhead. A voice broke around me and a long prayer of healing was read by what I assumed was a nun. It dawned on me that it was a Catholic hospital and that perhaps the prayer was a routine deal. Just then the door from the stairwell opened and a resident emerged.

"What's going on?" I asked, pointing up as though my finger was directly poised at the speaking nun.

"Nightly prayer," the man said. "They pray for healing each night."

"Wow, all that heaven will allow," I said.

The man shuffled off down the hall and away from me. I considered Jeff and his personal beliefs. There were so many moments when Jeff was reflective and considerate of others.

In late August of 2003, the entire town of North Collins suffered a tremendous loss as Heather Cataldo, a young girl who'd fought a courageous battle against a brain tumor, lost her life. The passing of Heather was extremely devastating to our entire family because the Cataldos, through the years, had shared in so much of our family life.

Heather's grandparents, Nado and Marge, were close friends of our Mom and Dad. John and Mary, Heather's parents, were there for the great times as we grew up together.

Heather passed just weeks after Jeff's daughter, Farrah's baptism, and the extremes of life shook Jeff to the very core. After attending Heather's wake, Jeff and I stopped at a bar near his home for a quick beer and a shot of Jameson.

"I don't get it," Jeff said as he raised his shot glass in a toast. "I feel so bad for Johnny and Mary. There can't possibly be a worse pain than losing your child."

"I have no idea how you'd possibly get through something like that," I said.

Jeff shook his head and ordered another round of shots. "I'd have to crawl into a bottle," he said.

"That probably wouldn't take away the pain," I said.

We had another drink. We spoke of the Alffs, the McGraths, the Lawtons, the Cammaratas, the Tezyks, the Hortons and the Bly families. All these wonderful families had been shaken to the core by the loss of a child.

"I want to build a moat around my property to protect my kids," Jeff said.

"That probably won't work either," I said. "Life gets in the way."

We lifted our glasses one more time. Through the years I'd grown used to the Irish limericks or truly tasteless jokes that accompanied a raised glass. Jeff surprised me that night.

"Thy will be done," he said.

Chapter VIII – Walk Like a Man

February 12-February 13, 2009 For it was not into my ear you whispered, but into my heart. It was not my lips you kissed, but my soul. Judy Garland

If love were to have a face, it most certainly would have a mother's eyes. During the workday on February 12 I ducked into the hospital during my lunch hour to find Mom sitting at the bedside. She glanced up at me as I entered the room and the look of despair on her face nearly dropped me to my knees. "How's he doing?" I whispered.

My mother shrugged and her eyes, those ever-loving eyes, threatened tears. She couldn't find the voice to answer me.

"Has he been sleeping a lot?" I asked.

 Mom nodded. "And coughing too. He's in a lot of pain when he coughs."

I walked to the other side of the bed. Jeff was holding a stuffed animal that belonged to his boy Rocco. It was a light brown bear that looked worn from hundreds of hugs, and the sight of the bear in the crook of his arm nearly sent me into a sobbing fit that would strip me of any chance of helping my mother cope with what was happening.

"Hey, buddy," I said.

"He hasn't been awake at all," Mom whispered.

"He was waiting for me," I said with a smile.

For a long while we sat in the quiet, but all at once, Jeff went into a coughing fit that raised him off the bed. The pain contorted his face, and I would have seen my mother look away if I hadn't been looking away myself. Yet when the coughing spasm ended, Jeff opened his eyes.

"Just relax, buddy," I said. "Squeeze my hand."

Jeff gave me a strong squeeze.

"That's my boy," I said. "You have another day of rest in the bank. You're doing great. You're healing. I know it's taking a lot of time, but you'll come around. Trust me."

Jeff's eyes were drooping and I was sure that he didn't get the message, but the words were mostly for Mom.

"Do you want a coffee or something?" I asked Mom when it became apparent that Jeff was heading back to a long sleep.

She shook her head. "I just want to sit here."

My quick afternoon visit did little to help my mood. I headed back to work thinking of my mother and father and all they'd done through the years to make sure that we were healthy and happy and well-fed. They'd sacrificed everything in their lives for the sake of their children, and it was more than a little disturbing to imagine what they were going through. I had felt that pain when my own son was in a life-threatening situation. I had prayed so hard during those days that I thought I'd break the blood vessels behind my eyes. My mother didn't have to say it to me as we sat on opposite sides of that bed, but I knew that she'd give her life to change what was happening.

As I worked that afternoon, the pain in my heart was doubled by the memory of growing up in a wonderfully loving home.

The look of love on the face of a mother is rivaled only by the proud expression of a loving father. There are moments in this life when we are allowed a glimpse of heaven. When Jeffrey Frank Fazzolari took his first breath of air, at 1:37 a.m. on June 22nd in 1970, John and Lynda Fazzolari felt pure, unadulterated love for the fifth time as parents.

Jeffrey was born at Children's Hospital of Buffalo, weighing in at eight pounds and seven ounces and twenty-one inches long. Mother and child were moved into room 210 for a few days before Jeffrey headed for home.

And what a home it was! The ever-growing Fazzolari family had settled into a beautiful house in North Collins, New York, a small town about twenty miles south of the city of Buffalo.

The home was expertly situated high on a hill in the quiet, serene town. The home was the vision of our parents and was built on the sweat, blood and tears of the entire family. Our father, John, with the help of his friends, parents, in-laws, uncles and cousins, had designed and assembled the home with love and years of happiness in mind. Our mother, Lynda, had certainly done her part in those early days by working hard to take care of all the children.

Of course, as parents of six children separated by a mere ten years, the joy of life was a bit lost on Mom and Dad. There were diapers to change, dinners to prepare, sleepless nights, out-of-town jobs, fights between the siblings, a couple of dogs tossed in for good measure and healthy doses of education, discipline and joy. More than anything else, there was very little rest as John and Lynda worked, worked and worked some more to build a family on a foundation of love, faith, hope and togetherness. As the ensuing years showed, they had the perfect recipe, including a future executive chef.

Through the formative years, in a family with six children, hardly a day went by when something didn't happen. Each day there was a chance that the powder keg could explode. One kid might argue with another over space, toys or food. The parents struggled just to gain some semblance of control over the everyday situation and most likely hung on for dear life at the end of each

A funny thing happened in the Fazzolari family. Through the years, not only was there a strong parental presence, but the children very often also slipped into roles as caretakers for one another. Corinne and Carrie were inseparable as they tried to shield themselves from the chaos of the four boys in between them. John and Jim spent a lot of time together, shadowing Dad as work was completed around the yard, on the cars and in the garage. Jeff and I tried hard to stay clear of most of the useful things that could get your hands dirty, concentrating instead on playing sports and having fun. Yet at any given moment it was known that one sibling or another could certainly slide over to become an ally with another sibling. Which brother or sister you were closest to often changed on a daily basis.

Looking back on my childhood, I can barely comprehend how two people could possibly raise six children who were so close in age. Some thirty years later, as adults, we would all marvel at the fact that we made it through unscathed. My mother often cried out for just a few moments of peace. As I tried hard to recall some of the days long ago, I went directly to the source, asking my mother to share a few of her memories of the relationship between her two youngest children. As we sipped coffee at the home where we all grew up, Mom and I spoke of those formative years.

Jeff and Carrie were close in age and even closer as brother and sister. The early years of their lives often found them together as though they were twins rather than siblings separated by two years. Of course, being together all the time often put Carrie in a dangerous position.

"I had no idea where they'd run off to," Mom said, "but I knew it was too quiet. In those days a couple of minutes of peace was rare. Yet it was going on too long, so finally I went looking for them. I opened Carrie's bedroom door and they were both in there, naked, and painting each other with nail polish. They were covered from head to toe and they were laughing their asses off. It took me a couple of hours to get them cleaned up."

Still, Mom just couldn't be everywhere.

"Then there was the time when Jeff gave Carrie a haircut. Somehow he got hold of a pair of scissors, and he chopped off her hair until she was just about bald."

Mom looked away as she recounted the stories. All at once, a smile overtook her. "There was the night when Jeff and Carrie watched the movie The Shining with Jack Nicholson. I had no idea that they had watched the movie, but Carrie was scared out of her mind. It was worse the next day when she returned to her bedroom to find that Jeff had scrawled the word 'REDRUM' across her mirror."

Looking back, there was no denying the mischief, but looking into my mother's eyes, I knew that she wouldn't have wanted it to play out any other way.

One of the true lessons learned in life was that if there were to be success, there would have to be hard work. Our parents taught us this lesson through simple demonstration. Dad was usually up and out of the house before the sun rose, and Mom started working shortly after that and didn't stop until long after we had all turned in for the night.

Growing up, it was hard to pinpoint even a single day when the washing machine wasn't turning or the vacuum wasn't running. If Dad was the hardest working guy in the construction world outside our doors, Mom put that work ethic to shame inside our home. As children, we learned to work. Whether we were doing our schoolwork or simply playing a game, we were striving to be the best.

Living within the confines of our huge family, there was love at every turn. Mom prepared dinner every day. Dad was ready and willing to provide discipline, humor and unpredictability. Both parents provided the hugs, kisses and security that we all needed. As growing children, we were intent on mimicking the steps of a mother and father who were teaching us the right way to walk.

During the course of the day on February 12, news broke about a horrific crime in western New York. A local man was accused of beheading his wife in a most shocking murder. When I returned to the hospital for the evening shift, the horrible crime was being discussed in the waiting room. Many of Jeff's friends had visited through the day, including Brad Gier, Kim Peterson and Mary Cataldo. Our cousin Tony had also made the long drive from his home in Gasport. Jim was speaking about the crime with a man I'd seen in the halls of the hospital but had not previously met.

"This is Dave White," Jim said.

I shook Dave's hand. "I've seen you here every day," I said. "I'm guessing you'd rather be somewhere else, too."

Dave had long salt-and-pepper hair that was tied back in a ponytail. Despite his tired eyes, he flashed a wry smile. "My brother's in the room across the hall from your brother, but my brother isn't coming home. We have to make a decision soon."

"Oh, man, I'm sorry," I said.

The smile faded and I saw that Dave's face was a mask of fatigue. He gave me a "what can you do?" look, and I flashed one back at him. Yet just a few minutes later, we were discussing the events of the day as if we'd known each other all of our lives. Even as we spoke of the crime in our own backyard, I was busy reflecting on the fact that each day a family was wracked with the same pain that we were feeling as a group. Our hearts went out to Dave on that evening, as we shared a bond that human beings should never be asked to share, but one that we all do.

Jim and John broke away for the evening, promising to be back in the morning. We were all trying so hard to maximize one another's rest time that we were overlapping the shifts and staying longer than we should have. Corinne and Chuck were also putting in eternally long hours, and Lynn suffered worst of all as she tried to visit as much as possible and also tried hard to keep life normal for her three small children. I thought of Lynn as Jim and John headed to the elevators, and I dialed her number. I wasn't ready for the voice that greeted me on the other end of the line.

"Hello, who is this?" three-year-old Rocco said.

"Hey buddy, it's Uncle Cliff. What're you doing?"

"I'm playing with Farrah," Rocco said. "Here's Mommy."

Lynn and I spoke for a few minutes, each offering support to the other. I had no way of knowing what she was going through because the pain in my own heart was so strong. Still, I offered to do anything in my power to help, and my dear sister-in-law responded in kind. We were helpless to give the support that was truly needed, and that was obviously the most frustrating aspect of our interaction. Lynn wanted her husband back. We wanted our brother, son and uncle back, and despite our overwhelming love, it wasn't happening fast enough.

"He'll be fine," I said. "Thank you for hanging that prayer in his room. It's helped me."

"Prayer is the only thing keeping me sane," Lynn said.

"Thanks for letting me hear Rocco's voice," I said. "Take care of those guys."

"I will," Lynn said.

Clicking the phone off after our good-bye I couldn't help but consider Jeff and Lynn and the day when I knew that Jeff was in love. I headed back to the waiting room, lowered myself onto the hard chair and thought back on the first time that I'd seen Lynn's face.

Just a couple of months before Jeff was to leave for school he called me early on a Friday afternoon. "Are you still at work?" he asked.

"Yeah, I'm done soon," I said. I was working in downtown Buffalo that afternoon and Jeff knew it.

"I'm thirsty," he said. "I'll meet you at The Pier."

The Pier was a bar and restaurant that did a bustling happy hour on the shore of Lake Erie. I wasn't sure if I was all that thrilled about fighting the crowd for a drink. I preferred a drink at the Malamute Bar in Buffalo where I could talk quietly with friends.

"I'm not going down there," I said.

"I need you to," Jeff said. "I want you to meet Lynn."

"Why do you want me to meet her?" I asked.

Jeff had dated a few girls through the years but he'd never made a special arrangement to have me meet with any of them. "She's pretty cool," he said. "You're going to like her."

Just a little while later when I entered The Pier, I was stunned by what I saw. Jeff was waiting for me and he was as dressed up as he ever seemed to get. Plus, he was definitely wearing cologne. I offered to buy him a shot of tequila.

"Nah, I'm going light tonight. I want you to meet Lynn."

"Well, where is she?" I asked. "I can't wait to bust her chops."

There was something different about Jeff that afternoon. "Go easy on her, would you?" he asked. "She might be it, man. I kind of like her."

I followed Jeff to a table where a very attractive brunette was sitting. He sat down next to her and very casually introduced her to me. "Cliff, this is Lynn. Lynn, Cliff, my bro."

I had planned to make fun of her to pay Jeff back for all of the craziness he'd put me through for years. Instead, I was astonished by what came out of my mouth.

"Dude, she's pretty!" I said.

I don't remember spending a lot of time at the table that night, but I do remember heading to my apartment just a few blocks away. During the short drive I considered what was really happening. My little brother was growing up.

Years later, as I drove to the hospital at five a.m. on the morning of February 13, I couldn't help but wonder, given my current state of mind, if the whole world was in the process of coming apart. The radio stations were broadcasting news of a late-night plane crash in Clarence, New York, not twenty miles from my home. Continental flight 3407 had crashed upon descent, and at least fifty people were dead.

"What the hell is happening?" I asked the interior of my car. "Jeff's sick, people are beheading each other and planes are falling from the sky. What the hell is next, God? Locusts?"

Deep down I knew enough to figure out that it wasn't God bringing the wrath, but I was tired, and I was sick of the violence and sadness. I needed some good news.

When I arrived at the hospital, the halls were quiet, and Jeff's room was dark. I peeked my head in, but when he coughed, I ducked back out and headed for the nurse's station.

"How'd he do overnight?" I asked.

"He's doing fine," the nurse said. "He's been sleeping a lot."

It wasn't the news I'd been looking for, but at least he'd rested. I moved down the hall to the waiting room and clicked on the overhead television set to learn the details of the plane crash. CNN was covering the news, showing footage of the tragedy. The elevator dinged to announce an arrival on the floor, and I moved to the front of the room, almost expecting to see a Fazzolari step through the doors. I wasn't disappointed either as Jim emerged carrying a bag from Tim Horton's. "I got you a breakfast sandwich," he said.

When Jim got within ten feet of me I was nearly over-come by the noxious odor coming from him. "Dude, you smell like shit," I said.

"Yeah, you smell that?" he asked. He handed me a sandwich and a coffee and then lifted his right foot. A huge clump of dog crap fell from his shoe onto the car-peted floor of the waiting room.

Truth be known, Jim has the weakest stomach of any man I'd ever met, and he began to choke and gag as tears of laughter ran down my cheeks. He plopped down on a chair and began feverishly wiping his feet on the brown carpet.

"Great idea!" I cried out. "Now you can sit and smell it the rest of the day."

Before long we were both standing in the hallway, laughing our way through the coffee. Neither one of us had yet garnered the stomach to eat the sandwich.

"You have to find someone to clean that up," Jim said.

"I'm going to go and see Jeff first," I said. "But I'll stop by the nurse's station on the way in."

As I headed down the hall, I thought of all of the laughs we'd had together through the years. Jim, Carrie, Corinne, John and Jeff were certainly my best friends in the world, and the fact that they were was a testament to the love we'd grown to appreciate. Yet for the next half an hour, after reporting the accident to the nurse's station, I thought of Jim's wedding and stag party and the fact that Jeff had been the star of the show.

As he prepared for his wedding Jim explained that he

wasn't much interested in the traditional stag party, but Jeff was determined to see that his brother's bachelor days ended in spectacular fashion. Jim's best buddies were contacted and Jeff made arrangements with a local golf course to accommodate the group.

The early Saturday morning meeting in the parking lot of the golf course was a chance to go over the rules for the outing as well as a chance to divide up the beer for the day. Jeff was paired with Jim and they teed off first. I shared a cart with my buddy Chris Heinold, and we were the second foursome out.

"This is going to be an absolute mess," Chris said as he loaded the beer into our cart.

That was certainly the understatement of the year.

Golfing with Jeff through the years was certainly an exercise in patience. At nearly every hole it was extremely important to check the strap holding your bag to the golf cart. Deftly, Jeff would sneak behind the cart and loosen the strap, and when your cart was moved, the bag would flop to the ground, resulting in a spilled bag and a hearty laugh. Before leaving the parking lot, Jeff made our cousin Tony the first victim of the day.

Yet his tricks were not confined to just the cart. He would lift your golf ball off the fairway and put it into his bag and laugh as you searched for it. He would shout in the middle of your backswing, laugh when you missed the short putt and stick his club into extremely sensitive places just as you were about to make contact with the ball. On the day of Jim's stag, all of his best tricks were on display.

At hole one, Chris nearly fell off the cart as he laughed at the message that Jeff had neatly inscribed in the sand trap closest to the green. Cliff is a fat bastard.

"We're going to get thrown out of here," I moaned as Chris continued to laugh.

"What did you expect?" Chris asked. "He's happy to be home."

The beers were flying out of the coolers at a rapid pace. Jim and Jeff put on a show at nearly every hole, clubbing one another's ball into the woods, chipping balls at traffic going by, driving the cart at the birds, into the pond and onto the greens. I was growing a tad uncomfortable with the proceedings, but at each hole Jeff reminded me to relax and enjoy myself. After the first nine holes there was a real concern about whether or not the attendants were going to let us finish the round.

"We have a problem," Jeff said as the front nine concluded. He was sitting in the cart, a huge grin covering his face. "We're running low on beer."

"The store is right down the road," Jim said. "Go get some more."

Now, another man may have done things differently, but to Jeff the answer was obvious. He floored the golf cart and drove straight down the middle of the public road as everyone gathered for the event laughed. Ten minutes later he was back with a case of beer. The owner of the course came screaming out of the clubhouse. "You can't take the golf cart off the course!" he yelled.

"I'll handle this," Jeff said.

I was actually in the process of loading my clubs back into the car, sure that we were going to be shown the exit. Instead, Jeff greeted the owner a couple of hundred feet from where we were gathered. We'll never know exactly what was said in the exchange, but one minute into the conversation the owner wrapped an arm around Jeff's shoulder as his face contorted in laughter.

"How does he get away with this crap?" I asked Chris.

"Everyone loves him," Chris said. "How can you not?"

The next couple of hours were a blur of beer, laughter and bad golf. When we finally reached the 18th hole, I was exhausted, a little loaded and in a hurry to get it over with.

I struck my drive to the center of the fairway. Jeff and Jim were completing their round, and Chris and I fully expected that they would razz us as we made our way up the final fairway. Razzing us would have been a welcome event. Rather than just yelling out insults, Jim and Jeff had other ideas.

"What're they doing?" I asked Chris.

"Looks like they're teeing up," Chris said. "Could it be?"

The first ball sailed directly over our heads.

"What the hell? They're hitting balls at us!" I screamed.

Chris scrambled to grab his ball as Jim's shot ripped into the cart. Hoots of laughter carried down the fairway as Chris and I jumped for cover. We never even finished the round and the rest of the stag party is better left to the memories of those in attendance that day. Suffice it to say, it was an event for the ages.

A couple of weeks later, Jeff stood before the gathering at Jim and Lisa's wedding reception. As expected, the speech that he delivered was touching and comical.

"It's an honor to have been chosen as the best man for Jim and Lisa's wedding. Of course, as I began collecting my thoughts about the kind of man that Jim has been, I realized that you might get the impression that Jim is a little bit insane.

"First of all, when Jim was just a little boy, he gave everyone a good scare when he ran into the kitchen to tell my father the score of the Yankee game. He tripped over the leg of a chair and struck his head on the kitchen table. Two things came of the incident: Jim developed a Frankenstein-like scar on his forehead, and it was also the last time that anyone ever saw him run.

"From there, Jim did a few things that must be considered strange. There was the time that he swallowed a Fred Flintstone pin and when they took the X-ray you could clearly see Dino's face smiling out from its spot in Jim's colon. My poor sister, Corinne, had to follow Jim into the bathroom for about a week to make sure he passed the pin.

"Then there was the scare he gave us when he decided to see what gasoline tasted like. The most upsetting thing was that he was rushed to the hospital for that little stunt: twice! He actually tasted it twice.

"Who can forget that Jim was the boy who bit the head off of a frog, threw a spit wad at his English teacher (it was so big and hard that it nearly killed her), got caught speeding in his Ford Galaxy (he was clocked going 136 mph), and nearly decapitated me with a baseball bat because I had the audacity to argue with him about a base hit. My mother watched the entire incident unfold.

"And then he met Lisa and Lisa's son, Adam. To let you know how smoothly their courtship has gone, my father's best advice to Jim was to put wheels on the television set because it had more miles on it then his car, as he moved it in and out of Lisa's home. Every man in this wedding party has had a conversation with Jim that has ended with him saying, 'I'm done, boy.'

"Yet while we've all seen the crazy side of Jim and Lisa, we've also seen the caring side. Jim has a heart the size of his head, and if anyone in the family needs help, he's always right there. He works hard, plays hard and spends money faster than the federal government.

"My final story concerns the look on Jim's face when he watched me try to flip my parent's car into their driveway. When Jim looked at me, all of the insanity and craziness was gone. His face was as white as a ghost's and I swear I saw tears in his eyes.

"So here we are. We're all overjoyed that Jim is now Lisa's problem.

"Jim, you're getting a beautiful, intelligent, caring girl. Love her with everything you have. You're also getting Adam, a smart, wonderful boy. Help him to grow in all of the ways that you did.

"Here is to Jim and Lisa! As Bruce Springsteen once said, 'God have mercy on the man who doubts what he's sure of.'

"Congratulations!"

On that cold day in February, I emerged from Jeff's room and rejoined Jim in the waiting room. He'd finished his sandwich, and evidently the staff had stopped by because there was a pine scent in the air. Jim, however, couldn't control a fit of laughter that was shaking his entire body.

"What?" I asked. "They came and cleaned it, right?"

"Yeah, it was an older lady and she was gagging the entire time. She kept saying, 'I've never in all my years seen anything like this.'"

It was no exaggeration, but neither Jim nor I had laughed so hard in weeks.

"Finally she couldn't take anymore and she asked me, 'Where did this come from?'"

Jim was holding his stomach as his face went a couple of shades of red with glee.

"I told her, 'I think it's that filthy pig that sleeps in here at night,' and she said, 'That's exactly what I was thinking.'"

We laughed even harder, and without even saying it, we both had the same exact thought: We couldn't wait to tell the story to Jeff.

Chapter IX – Human Touch

February 14-February 16, 2009   There are two ways to live; you can live as if nothing is a miracle; you can live as if everything is a miracle.   Albert Einstein

As a family, we were certainly scrambling with Jeff's illness, his long bouts of sleep and the long-term prognosis. Our ability to make one another laugh was being hampered by the fact that the funniest man we knew was waking up for just minutes at a time. Additionally, there was just so much misinformation mingled with the frustration that, one by one, we were all in need of a mental break, but there wasn't one on the immediate horizon. We tried hard to make our own breaks.

On Friday night, Corinne and Chuck, along with John and Dana, settled in for a long evening at the hospital, and they issued strict instructions to me. I was to stay away, try to relax and have a few drinks if necessary. I saw no other option then to take them up on their instruction.

I commissioned my good buddy Chris Miller to join me for a couple of dirty martinis at the local bar, and Chris was only too willing to provide me with a little company and a ton of perspective. We hunkered down in a quiet tavern and ordered Grey Goose. Chris was the perfect companion for the evening, but one of the first things he asked me to do was recap the famous story of my trip with Jeff to an NCAA basketball game in West Virginia. I was only too happy to regale him with the story.

On a cold day in February of 1992, Jeff agreed to join me for a trip from Buffalo to Morgantown, West Virginia, for an NCAA women's basketball game. A friend of mine,

Rosemary, was an All-American guard playing on the West Virginia team. I had enticed Jeff to go by saying that I would pay for the hotel room and that we could grab a few beers with Rosemary and her boyfriend, Doug.

"Why not? I've never seen a woman's basketball game," Jeff said.

The plan was for him to meet me at my apartment. I was scrambling to get everything done, and I left Jeff in the apartment alone as I filled the car with gas. To my surprise, he met me at the curb, holding both of our suitcases. Ten minutes later, we were on the road.

As the driver, my duty was to watch the road and allow Jeff to handle the tunes. He popped Springsteen's The Wild and the Innocent into the cassette player, and we listened, sang, talked Bruce and shared stories of work, family and life. About an hour into the trip, Jeff reached into the back seat and removed two beers.

"You drinking?" he asked.

"I'm driving," I said.

"You don't mind if I have a beverage, do you?"

"Be your own man," I said.

For the next hour and a half, I drove and Jeff drank, sang, pretended he was going to tickle me and kidded me about anything that came to his mind.

We arrived in Morgantown just before game time. Rosemary was already on the court, but she knew that we were planning to attend and she glanced up to our seats and offered a wave. By now, Jeff was in great spirits. "She likes you," he said. "She waved! Doesn't that excite you?"

The place was a sell-out. The game was a competitive battle with my friend at the center of it all. Rosemary was scoring points, dishing the ball to her teammates and racing up and down the court.

"She's good," Jeff finally admitted.

At halftime we hit the restroom. Jeff and I worked our way through a packed room, ending up next to each other at the urinals. I wasn't thinking about it much but when I looked up at him, he smiled.

Uh-oh, I thought.

"What're you looking at?" Jeff screamed out. The packed room went dead silent.

"This guy's staring at me!" he yelled.

"Knock it off," I whispered.

"You're some kind of pervert!" Jeff yelled.

He turned to the stunned crowd of men standing ten-deep behind us. I was trying my best to pee as fast as I could.

"I caught him peeking!" Jeff squealed.

Before I could take more than three steps away, my face flushed with embarrassment, he clasped an arm around my shoulder.

"I think I'll take him home!" Jeff yelled. I think I was the only one in the room who caught his subtle wink.

Yet the evening took an even stranger turn after we had grabbed a bite to eat with Rosemary and Doug. Jeff and I headed to the hotel room, our bags in tow. "I just can't wait to take a shower and get into bed," I said.

"You might have to go out again," Jeff said.

"What the hell are you talking about? I'm done," I said.

I sat down on the bed closest to the door. Jeff sat with his knees just a few feet away from me on the other bed. He was offering the most sinister of smiles, but I wasn't having anything of it.

"Will you give me a break?" I said. "I'm tired."

I put my suitcase on my lap and unzipped it. Jeff still hadn't moved, and although he was seriously crowding me, I wasn't going to give him the satisfaction of knowing that he was getting under my skin.

I started digging through my suitcase, looking for a

clean pair of undershorts and a shirt to wear to bed. The first handful of clothes that I pulled out was socks. There were at least twenty pairs.

"What the hell?" I asked.

I unzipped another compartment, reached again and pulled out…more socks. It was then that I bothered to look up. Jeff was now just inches from my face.

"Problem?" he asked.

It still hadn't registered. I was just so tired that I was in that space where I believed that I was just imagining things. I stood up, laid the case flat on the bed and opened every compartment, not finding any other article of clothing other than every sock I owned.

"I know I packed," I said, and as the words left my mouth I considered that I had left him alone in the apartment with my packed suitcase.

"I'd let you borrow a pair of pants," he said, "but you're too fat."

"You bastard!" I yelled. "There isn't even anyone here to enjoy the joke!"

"I'm enjoying it," he said. "We passed a K-Mart about a mile back. If I'm sleeping when you get back, please try to be considerate."

I closed the door and headed to K-Mart to buy clothes. I was seething when I left and laughing hard as I walked the aisles, searching for new clothes.

That walking celebration had got me good.

Chris laughed all the way through the story. We refilled our glasses and toasted Jeff.

"The thing about Jeff is that he lived every day as though it was going to be his last," Chris said. "We just need him to have a million more. That's not too much to ask, is it?"

"I don't think so," I said.

"It's a good lesson for everyone who loves him though,

don't you think?" Chris asked.

"I didn't need this lesson," I said.

"Life isn't the day-to-day crap we put up with," Chris said. "Life is the stuff that happens that we aren't pre-pared for."

Two drinks in, I no longer wanted to be at the bar. I headed to the men's room where, in the quiet stall, I used my cell phone to dial Corinne at the bedside.

"He's doing okay," Corinne said. "He just thumb-wres-tled with Pops, and even though his temperature is a little high, he's been awake some. The doctors are talk-ing about removing the trach tube and finally setting the feeding tube into his stomach. The next time you see him his face might be clear of tubes. Now go back and have a drink for me. Nurse Corinne and Nurse Dana are on duty!"

I headed back to the bar feeling a little better about the next few hours, and Chris was more than happy to line up the next round of drinks.

"He'll make it through," Chris said. "It isn't going to be as easy as we might need it to be, but we'll get through it."

I raised my glass in a toast. "To the walking celebra-tion," I said. "Did I ever tell you what he did to me in Florida?"

Chris clanked glasses with me. "Give it to me," he said. "I'm sure it's a beauty."

I took a sip of my drink, leaned on the bar for support and started telling him the story.
***

The discussion of possibly going on vacation started in September of 1989. Jeff was working as a bricklayer on a construction job and, with a mind to start college in late January, he wanted one last big fling before the aggrava-tion began.

"Come on, bro, let's go to Florida for a couple of weeks," he begged. "I got a couple hundred bucks saved up. We can live like kings."

I had recently completed a long working stint away from home having just returned from an eight-month project in New Haven, Connecticut. "I don't want to go to Florida," I told Jeff.

"You'll want to go in January," he said, "when you're up to your ass in snow."

"If you come to me with a plan, I'll think about it," I said.

Two days later, Jeff busted into the writing office I'd set up in my parent's basement. "Oh, you're here!" he said.

His face was home to a wicked smile, and casually, he palmed my American Express Card, pretending that he was hiding it under one of my notebooks. All the while he was looking at my face and smiling.

"We're all set," he said.

"Set for what?" I asked.

"We're going to Fort Meyers for two weeks. I booked us a great hotel on the water, and I set up the rental car. This vacation is a little pricey, but we'll be just fine."

"What're you talking about? What did you do?"

"Hang on, hang on, hang on," Jeff said as he ran through the basement, up the stairs and out into the garage. Moments later, he was back with two bottles of beer and a folding chair.

"The airline tickets were easy," he said. "You have a sign and travel option on the AMEX that is interest-free for three months. We'll pay that off in no time. The hotel was a bit more of a problem because I didn't want any rat-trap places, you know? We needed to get something with a kitchen so I can cook for us."

Jeff took a huge swig of the beer and motioned to the one he'd opened for me. He swallowed hard for dramatic effect and smiled. "This is going to be easier for you to take if you sip your beer," he said.

"You did not book everything without asking me." I said.

"I sure did," he said. "I know how busy you are pretending to be writing books, so I took the liberty. I just called and said I was Clifford J. Fazzolari." He smiled again and casually picked up the beer he'd brought for me. "Come on, have a sip. It's good."

"How much did you pay for the hotel?" I asked.

"How much did we pay for the hotel?" he corrected.

"And is this all on my credit card?"

"For now, my lovely brother, but I've already cut you a check for my half."

Jeff reached into his back pocket and fished out an already filled-out check. He pushed it across the desk, along with the information about the flight, the hotel and the rented car.

"I'll leave you to figure all that out," he said. "I know how intellectual you are, and how you'll want to go through it with a fine-tooth comb."

"You did not do this," I said.

"We're all set!"

Jeff reached across and tried tickling me and I pushed him away. He took great care in closing the door to the office and shushing himself as he shuffled away. "Be very, very quiet," he whispered. "Cliff has to study what Jeff did for him."

I didn't want to laugh so that he could hear me, and when I glanced at the information he'd scribbled on the yellow notepad my heart got stuck in my throat. He had booked a fairly expensive hotel, a mid-sized rental car and two airplane tickets, all on my credit card. I did a quick calculation, adding up the entire cost of the trip before I glanced at his check. He had written the check for fifty percent of the costs, right down to the penny.

I heard him clear his throat on the other side of the

door. "We're all set, right?" he called out.

"I suppose," I said.

Jeff opened the door and this time, he did tickle me. "Two weeks on the beach!" he said.

"Two weeks of putting up with your crap," I said.

"It's going to be awesome!"

Jeff swigged the rest of his beer and pointed to mine. "One little thing," he said.

"What?" I asked as I finally lifted the beer to my mouth.

"Don't try cashing that check for awhile," he said.

The flight to Florida was an extremely long and bumpy ride. Much of the difficulty in the journey was directly related to the fact that every sentence out of my mouth was greeted with the same sarcastic laugh that Jeff had perfected as a way to get under my skin, "A-ha-a-ha-a-ha-a-ha-a-ha," he would wail as loudly as he could.

"Please stop that," I whispered.

"You make me laugh," he said.

Growing weary with his constant teasing, I yawned. He stuck his finger in my mouth. "A-ha-a-ha-a-ha-a-ha-a-ha," he wailed.

"Is this how the whole trip is going to be?" I asked, spitting out his finger.

"Perhaps," he said, arching his eyebrows and smiling wide.

I had no idea how challenging the trip really would be.

On the first night of our stay in Fort Myers, I sat alone at the bar nursing a beer. Jeff had disappeared into the back room to shoot pool with a few guys he'd just met. About half an hour later, the bouncer pointed to me across the crowded bar. The big, burly man came to me in a near sprint and immediately poked me in the center of the chest. I couldn't help but stare at the huge tattoo covering his left arm. "Get your brother and get out!" the bouncer growled.

I headed into the back room where Jeff was shooting pool and doing his "A-ha-a-ha-a-ha-a-ha-a-ha," to the patrons. There were two cigarettes dangling from each side of his mouth. "Cliffy!" he yelled when I entered the room.

"We have to go," I said.

"No, no, meet my friends," he said.

I removed both cigarettes from his lips and led him to the door. We passed the huge bouncer with the tattooed arms and Jeff smiled at him. "You have a great night!" he yelled.

Once out on the sidewalk I noticed that Jeff wasn't quite as drunk as he had been acting.

"Don't yell at me," he said. "I was just trying to entertain a few people. I guess they didn't like my a-ha-a-ha-a-ha-a-ha-a-ha laugh."

"Dude, it is a tad annoying," I said.

As we walked back toward the hotel room, his raucous mood was replaced by a contemplative stare. "People don't know how to have fun," he said. "That bouncer came running because there was a girl in there who didn't like the way I was laughing. Can you imagine?"

"As I've said, it can get a bit annoying."

"Yeah, but you know, we only get one chance to live every day. Why don't people just relax?"

I knew that it was a chance to impart a little bit of wisdom. Jeff had always looked up to me, and in a way I felt responsible for everything he did. I wasn't angry that we'd been tossed from the bar, but as long as I had his ear I would give it the old college try. "You have to minimize your chances of being caught in a bad situation," I said. "No one will ever begrudge you your fun, but you have to be ready to face the consequences, and keeping yourself out of trouble is usually the best bet."

Jeff draped a long arm around my right shoulder. "A-ha-a-ha-a-ha-a-ha-a-ha," he laughed. "A-ha-a-ha-a-ha-a-ha-a-ha."

He promptly broke free from my grasp and disappeared behind a trash bin in the back lot of a convenience store.

"What're you doing?" I asked.

"Peeing," he called out.

"Minimize your chances!" I scolded.

There was a long pause and even though I couldn't see him in his spot behind the dumpster, I could certainly hear him.

"A-ha-a-ha-a-ha-a-ha-a-ha."

For the next two weeks we baked in the sun, rode jet skis, spent every extra nickel we had on beer, and, in a time before I-pods, sang songs accappella, trying to get the words right. I will never forget standing on the porch at the Day's Inn, taking turns singing Thunder Road by Springsteen, and We Didn't Start the Fire by Billy Joel. To this day, I believe that the only three people who ever got every word right in We Didn't Start the Fire were Jeff, me and, of course, Billy Joel.

Every night of the trip, Jeff cooked dinner for me in the kitchen in our suite. We had linguine and clams, rolled pork tenderloins, haddock in tomato sauce, steak and shrimp and lobster tails.

"Have you figured out what you want to do with your life?" I asked Jeff during one of those meals.

"Live on the beach and jet ski," he answered.

"I'm talking about a job," I said. "I'm thinking you could be a chef."

"I'm already a chef," he said. "I just need someone to pay me for it. Now eat up, brother, we have beer to drink."

On the last day of our vacation in Florida, Jeff was up and out of bed early. He was standing on the back porch with a steaming cup of coffee. He was looking out at the beach, softly singing a Billy Joel song to himself. I poured a cup of coffee and joined him on his spot on the porch.

"Good morning, sunshine!" he said. "You're going to make something out of yourself when you get rid of those bed sores."

"What're you doing?" I asked.

"Just thinking about today," he said. "I'm thinking we make it a day we never forget."

"Oh please," I said. I sipped my coffee and discovered that he had already been blessed with his idea of how to make the day unforgettable.

"We're going to shave our heads," he said, "and get us some shades. When we get off the plane we'll give Dad a heart attack."

"I'm not shaving my head," I said.

"A-ha-a-ha-a-ha-a-ha-a-ha," Jeff laughed. "Yes you are."

We returned the rental car and walked to a strip mall not far from the airport. I still had every hair on my head, but the constant reminder that I would soon be bald was ringing in my ears in the form of Jeff's voice.

"I'm not shaving my head."

We headed into a bookstore, as I was intent on just getting away from Jeff for a few moments and perhaps reading something on the trip home.

"I'll catch up with you in a few minutes," Jeff said.

I hadn't really minded that he had walked away. I leafed through the bargain books, finally settling on a Stephen King novel, and was at the cash register when I saw Jeff jumping up and down in the front window of the store.

"Oh, for God's sakes," I said under my breath.

Jeff waved his arms for me to join him, but when I stepped out onto the sidewalk, he was gone.

"Why?" I screamed. "Why does this kid torment me?"

Three doors down, I glanced into the front window of

the barbershop. Jeff was seated in the chair, and the barber had just made a long swoop with the razor. I dropped the bag with the book inside.

Five hours later we stepped off the plane in Buffalo. We wore dark shades, short pants and muscle shirts. Since the air temperature was about twenty-five degrees in Buffalo, we made a terrific sight. Of course, our heads were neatly shaved. On Jeff's coaxing, we walked right up to my father and took a bow.

"What the hell is the matter with you two?" my father asked as he took in our appearance.

"It was his idea," I said.

"Yeah, well, no shit," my father said. "You look like a couple of real idiots."

"We'll never forget this day," Jeff said. "A-ha-a-ha-a-ha-a-ha-a-ha."

When I finished the story, Chris and I headed for the door. It had felt great to loosen up a bit and share drinks with a good friend. Chris dropped me off at my front door and I hustled inside.

That night as I prepared for bed, Kathy came to me and offered a reassuring hug. Grey Goose and fatigue were clouding my mind and I finally let loose. "This is Jeff we're talking about!" I cried. "We can't lose Jeff!"

Kathy sat up for me for over an hour. We consoled one another through the tears. I couldn't imagine trying to battle the heartbreak without a great wife by my side. Yet for the first time, the alcohol afforded me the chance to let loose of some of the anger that was raging inside of me. How could Jeff get into this situation? Didn't he know that we all needed him to be healthy? Was it something he'd done? Was it God? Did God do this to test us?

"I don't need a fucking test," I growled at Kathy.

"It's no one's fault," Kathy said. "People get sick every day. It's just our turn to face it."

"But it's Jeff!" I cried.

I finally fell asleep, but despite the alcohol, I only tossed and turned for a few hours before I considered myself fit enough to make the trip to the hospital. I arrived at the doors of Mercy Hospital just a few minutes after 4 a.m. I made the automatic trip to the bank of elevators and punched the button for the ICU floor. I was still half asleep and my head hurt a little, but I figured that seeing Jeff with my own eyes would cure all that was ailing me. What I didn't expect was that I would be the third visitor to arrive at his door that morning. John and Jim were sitting together at the bedside.

"What're you guys doing here already?" I asked.

"Same thing as you," John said. "This is the only place where we feel comfortable."

Jeff, of course, was sleeping through it all, and although there was quiet in the room, we were all together again, just as we had been so many days before.

The three of us stayed by Jeff's side all through the morning, but before too long we were joined by family friends John and Kay Renzoni, Tom Rybak, nearly every member of the Bowman family and Fran Mahoney and Paul Rose from the Gow School. Jeff slept through each visit, and our frustration grew. If it weren't for the respiratory therapist, Frank Guido, we might have launched a revolution then and there.

Frank, a respected member of the hospital staff, wasn't even a member of Jeff's care team, but as a friend to Jeff's boss, Brad Rogers, at the Gow School, Frank made Jeff's well-being his business. Frank would stop in to check on Jeff and he would very often do the work of the nurses, suctioning Jeff, telling jokes to keep us at ease and treating us like a member of his own family.

"He's going to be all right," Frank told us. "This just takes time. Don't get down about it. Just keep doing what you're doing."

Frank offered more comfort than nearly all of the rest
of the staff combined, and on that dreary Saturday morn-
ing, he provided three lonely brothers with a ray of sun-
shine.

I headed out of the hospital at 3 p.m. Despite my
desire to stay at the bedside and never leave, I was
scheduled to attend the Hunter's Day of Hope Celebra-
tion at the Buffalo Bills field house. The celebration was
held in honor of Hunter Kelly, the son of Hall-of-Fame
quarterback Jim Kelly and his wife Jill. I was scheduled to
sign copies of the book, House of Miracles that I'd writ-
ten about the Women & Children's Hospital. A couple of
years prior, Jill had written a wonderful foreword to the
book, and I was honored to be a small part of the cel-
ebration. Besides, my boys loved running around the field
house, kicking field goals and catching passes thrown by
Jim Kelly and other former members of the Bills.

The Hunter's Hope Foundation, which does a won-
derful job of hosting the event each year, set up a table
for me so that I could sign books for the guests. I stood
behind the table, scanning the happy faces of the chil-
dren who'd gathered. Kathy and the boys were running
across the football field, catching long passes and laugh-
ing. I signed a couple of books, but for the first time in
my writing life, I was down in the dumps about making
an appearance, and that was because my number-one
fan wasn't going to step up in line and tell me that he was
proud of me. Through the years, Jeff had never missed
one of my local book signings, and standing in a field
house full of strangers, I actually felt a little ridiculous.
Having a best-selling book was no longer important. I
had been writing for the people I loved. Pure and simple,
it had always been about writing for the people I loved.
Standing in a crowd of people, I thought back to a couple

of book events that Jeff took control of, as only he could do.

As the year 2003 wound down, the long hours at his job created real havoc with Jeff's back. Despite all attempts to suck it up and tough it out, Jeff was forced by his doctor to take some time off to see if his back would heal with rest. He was suffering with badly damaged discs and a tumor that was wedged into a precarious spot on the spine. Standing and cooking hour after hour and day after day was akin to torture.

The doctor-ordered time-out was difficult for Jeff, as being laid-up was next to mission-impossible for him. The kids were on the move around his home, and he needed to continue to provide for them. Lynn was also hustling to hold everything together and, like all young parents, they were faced with long, challenging days. Still, Jeff found a bit of time to do his favorite thing: bust chops.

Appearing on live television isn't an easy thing to do. The first time I appeared on the show AM Buffalo in late 2000, I was pretty nervous, and I must admit that I stuttered my initial greeting.

When my book Counting on a Miracle was released, I was afforded another opportunity to appear on AM Buffalo. I prepared well for the appearance right down to the smallest detail, which was allowing my wife to pick out the clothes that I would wear. Kathy made a special trip to the store and picked a very colorful blue shirt that was completely opposite to my usual style of dress. I didn't argue. When it comes to style, my wife has it way over me.

The interview went well. I did not stumble over even a single word. The host, Linda Pellegrino, had me stay for two segments, and I was actually thrilled with how it all went down. Thrilled, that is, until the segment ended and I stepped from the stage. I was still shaking Linda's hand when my cell phone vibrated in my front pocket.

I hurried to the left of the stage and answered the call.

"Dude," Jeff said. "Did you lose a bet? Where in the hell did you get that shirt?"

"Kathy picked it out," I said.

"I could see your nipples through the cloth. I was ready to puke up my breakfast."

My heart was stuck firmly in my throat. Jeff hung up the phone without another word, and I raced home to catch the replay of my appearance as Kathy had taped it. The shirt hadn't looked that bad! Little did I know, Jeff had decided to start a trend. It was as if he were reminding me that if I were to put myself out there, I would have to live with the consequences.

A little more than two weeks later, I appeared on PM Buffalo, the afternoon version of the show. I was actually feeling good about the appearance, knowing that Kathy would make me look halfway decent and that I would be able to answer each and every question.

Once more, I stepped from the stage feeling as if I had nailed it. Two steps off the stage however, the cell phone vibrated in my front pocket.

"Dude, I realize that the camera adds ten pounds, but how many freaking cameras did they have on you?" Jeff asked.

The sounds of his laughter were quickly extinguished as I closed the phone.

Months later, I was invited to do a thirty-minute interview for WNY Live. The show was very important to me, as I was being allowed a good chunk of time to discuss the work at the Women & Children's Hospital of Buffalo. I wanted to trumpet the work of the doctors and nurses who had teamed up to save my son Jake's life. Ten minutes into the interview, I was thrown for a huge curve.

"What do you say we take a few live calls?" the host asked.

"Sure," I replied confidently, knowing that I could handle anything at that point. Instantly a line lit up and on the board above the host's head flashed a prompt that said, "Line one is, Jeff from Hamburg."

In a split second, my mind shifted from confidence to fear. I wanted to scream at the host, to warn her against picking up the line, but it was too late!

"Hello, Jeff from Hamburg," the host said. "Do you have a question for Cliff?"

"No," Jeff said. "I just want to comment that I can still see his nipples, and that the Yankees are winning four to two in the sixth."

I nearly fell off my chair as the host scrambled to regain solid footing.

"That's my brother," I mumbled. "He's my biggest fan."

The host laughed nervously as Jeff asked a follow-up question.

"How many cameras do you have on him?"

"What was that?" the host asked.

"Please hang up on him," I said.

As I drove to my home following the interview, I couldn't help but laugh. Although I was intent on getting my message out, Jeff was teaching me a life lesson: 'Don't take yourself too seriously.'

It was a lesson that was lost on me in the moment, but my "walking celebration" made each television appearance memorable.

As the book signing at the Hunter's Hope Celebration drew to a close Jill Kelly joined me at the side of the stage. I explained to Jill what had happened with Jeff, and she offered sympathy with a heart-felt hug that I sorely needed. Jill bent to take the hands of my boys, Jake and Sam.

"Come on, we have some work to do. Jeff likes the Bills, right?"

"Loves them," I said.

Slinking through the crowd, Jill used her influence to get Thurman Thomas and Jim Kelly to sign a football for Jeff.

"He's going to love that, right?" Sam asked. "Two Hall-of-Famers!"

I didn't answer my boy right away. Despite all that was happening, the human touch of dear friends was lifting me up when I was most down.

Chapter X – No Surrender

February 17-February 21, 2009   The Lord will be your ev-erlasting light, and your days of sorrow will end. ISA 60:20

As the week began, we finally felt as though we might be getting somewhere. The staff explained that by the end of the week, Jeff would be freed of the trach tube as well as the feed line on the tip of his nose. The staff was also planning to operate on Jeff to place a shunt in his brain that would help drain the fluid. The initial thought was that before too long, he'd be more awake and aware. There was even a discussion about getting him up and out of the bed in a couple of days. Yet I didn't feel much like jumping for joy.

At the outset of the trouble, I firmly believed that Jeff would be as good as new in just a matter of months. Day after day of seeing him sleep was shaking my confidence a little, and the idea that he would have to live with a shunt for the rest of his life was more than a little discon-certing. A telephone call from Lynn shook me to the very core.

"We may have to change our expectations," Lynn said. "The doctors have been pretty forthcoming in saying that the Jeff we used to know probably won't make it through this. They don't know how far he'll come back, but there will be damage."

"How can they say that?" I asked. "He's a strong guy."

Lynn was quiet for a long moment. She knew that she was delivering news that I didn't want to hear and that I might be ready and willing to shoot the messenger.

"I know he's strong," Lynn said. "But there is a chance that he may never work again. I have to prepare myself and the kids for that possibility."

"He's going to be back one hundred percent, you'll see," I said.

I wasn't sure if I was trying to comfort Lynn or convince myself, but I certainly didn't want any part of the negative talk. Jeff would be shooting hoops again. He would be preparing gourmet meals for hundreds of people. If the doctors thought otherwise, they were wrong! People lived long, productive lives with a shunt in their heads. I wasn't about to give up hope.

There was little improvement on Monday. Jeff was asleep for most of the day, occasionally raising an eyebrow or squeezing a hand or two, but much less animated than he had been over the last couple of weeks.

"Did something else happen?" my father asked me when I arrived on Tuesday morning.

"Not that I know of," I said. I handed him a coffee across the table.

"I've been here since 4 a.m." Dad said. "I've already had three cups of coffee."

Still, he accepted the coffee, removed the lid and stirred it with a pen. I was sort of looking to him for an answer, as I'd done all through my life, but Dad was silent.

"Perhaps the shunt will help him come around again," I said. "They most likely wanted to see if he could snap out of it on his own, but I guess they'll have to rely on me-chanical means."

"Yeah, maybe that's it. His eyes were open this morning, but it's so hard to even look at him."

Dad bowed his head. I lifted my coffee cup. We wanted so badly to console each other, but the words were hard to come by. Dad had never let any of us down. He had worked like a dog for most of his life.

"I'm going to check in on him," I said.

Dad didn't answer.

As I made the walk down the hall, I considered a day from long ago. It was a typical sort of day in the life of the man who sat alone, sipping coffee, waiting on an answer.

Before leaving for Norfolk, Virginia, to start the culinary arts program, Jeff had thought of everything. His last little bit of planning involved me. At that time, Jeff was driving a white Mercury Cougar that was his dream car in every way. Every way except for one, that is; the Cougar still had a heavy payment book.

During that time, I was driving a Ford Mustang that, while fully paid for, was on its last legs and certainly was no match for the Buffalo winters. Still, I no longer had to make a payment each month, and I was happy to be clear of the financial obligation.

"Let's switch cars," Jeff said. "While I'm at school I won't be able to afford the payments on the Cougar. We'll trade cars, you pick up the payments on the Cougar and I'll drive the Mustang until it dies."

"The Mustang is awful in the snow," I said. "You're going to be driving back and forth. Besides, I don't want a car payment."

Yet as usually happened, I could not deny Jeff. We transferred the ownership and made the trade. Three weeks later, the transmission went on the Mustang.

"Now I'm just plain screwed," Jeff explained.

Feeling absolutely responsible, I made plans to borrow money to help him pay for the transmission repairs. Yet I never had to give him a dime.

On the Saturday morning before Jeff was to leave, I got a phone call that drove me crazy.

"Dad needs us to do some work around the house," Jeff said. "He's been like a madman all day; you better come and help."

I climbed into my beautiful white Cougar and drove to the house. Jeff was already trimming the hedges. Jim was using the riding mower in the backyard and John was push-mowing in the tight spots. As usual, we were all helping out. Dad was nowhere to be seen, and I was thankful for at least that much. We would be able to work without him standing behind us, cracking the whip.

Our work took us the better part of a couple of hours and we headed into the house for a glass of cold water and a conversation with Mom, who was working harder than all of us combined as she cooked and cleaned. Dad strolled in and immediately began to growl.

"Come on, get out there and clean up the clippings in the driveway. All of you!"

Begrudgingly we headed out the door, each complaining that we couldn't ever do enough to please dear old Dad. Jeff was leading the charge out the front door when he stopped dead in his tracks and pointed to a shiny, dark blue Cougar parked in the middle of the drive.

"Whose car is that?" he asked.

"Yours," my father said as he placed the keys into the palm of Jeff's hand. "Did we ever let you down?"

Jeff actually gasped, and we all headed for the car, shaking our heads in disbelief.

"Now go to school and make us all proud," Dad said.

Looking back on it, it was certainly one of those perfect moments in life. Jeff drove that car until he was married, and he certainly lived up to his end of the bargain. He made Mom and Dad proud as hell.

Work was interfering with my ability to concentrate on Jeff's recovery. By 6 a.m. on Tuesday, John had arrived at the hospital, driving nearly a hundred miles after his work shift so that he could take a turn at Jeff's side. I spoke to John for just a few minutes before I jumped in my car and headed to Syracuse for the day. As I drove, I left the stereo off. I didn't want to listen to music. I certainly couldn't bear to hear Springsteen's voice. Instead, I gazed up at the gray skies.

"What the fuck God?" I screamed as I punched the roof of my car from my spot behind the steering wheel.

Two hours later, just before I arrived at my client's office, I took one more telephone call. Chuck was on the other end of the line; moments into the conversation I understood that he had called just to reassure me a little bit. "I'm heading into the hospital now," he said. "Corinne is going to spend the evening with Jeff, and Carrie is coming in for the weekend. He's going to be okay, you know?"

"I know," I said.

"It's easy to get discouraged, but we all have to dig even deeper."

Chuck's little pep talk did wonders for my immediate mood, and before I got out of the car I looked to the skies once more. "Sorry about the fuck question," I muttered. "I haven't given up yet."

I appreciated the presence of Chuck in my life, and of course, I thought back to how he had made his entrance into the family.

In 1984, the dynamic of the Fazzolari household was truly changing. As we grew together, so too did our bond to one another. Corinne and John began bringing dates around, and very often there would be another plate set at the dinner table. The relative stranger to the table was usually caught wide-eyed and staring in the direction of Jeff, who did all he could to make the newcomer uncomfortable.

Unbeknownst to all but Corinne, one man who entered our lives would pass the orientation, indoctrination and all of the simple tests. Charles Leone began dating Corinne and despite a rough welcome, he proved he was in for the long haul. To hear Chuck tell the story, his integration certainly wasn't easy.

"The first time I met your father, he playfully slapped me across the face and said 'That's for dating my daughter,'" Chuck said. "Jeffrey pulled up a chair and sat so close that I could feel his breath. He sat there for two hours, just scanning me from head to toe, not saying even a single word. He looked at my hair for a long while, and every once in awhile he would shake his head as though he was in complete disapproval. I should have run, but I never did."

Chuck didn't beat-feet for the door. Instead he was accepted as a brother and, like each and every one of us, he considered Jeff among his very best friends, even after the pool incident.

One Sunday afternoon in the dead of summer, Chuck showed up at the house as an invited guest for pasta. The visit was just a few months after Corinne and Chuck had begun dating, so he was a tad apprehensive about what might happen. Yet for one reason or another, he trusted me.

Corinne poured a glass of iced tea for Chuck and the three of us sat at the kitchen table, sipping tea and talking about everything from NASCAR to the Yankees' chances of competing.

The commotion started when John and Jim hustled into the house and grabbed hold of me, just as we had planned.

"You're going in the pool!" John announced as he lifted me out of the chair.

I did my very best acting job, screaming and pleading for help. "Chuck! Help me!"

My two brothers carried me out of the house and onto the back porch.

"Help!" I screamed in Chuck's direction, and the poor bastard took the bait.

Just as we reached the pool's edge, Jeff emerged from

behind a bush. Jim and John let me down and together all four brothers scooped Chuck into the air.

Despite the fact that Chuck was dressed in jeans and a nice shirt, regardless of the watch that was dangling from his wrist and in spite of his protests to allow him to remove his glasses, we dropped him in the deep end of the pool.

"Welcome to the family!" Jeff squealed.

And still Chuck did not run.

For over twelve years I've been visiting the offices of Raulli & Sons, a steel erector and fabricator based in Syracuse. In those twelve years I'd made friends with all of the Raulli employees, and every visit was more like a social event then a work detail. As I entered the offices on that cold February morning, however, I was dreading having to talk about Jeff's battle.

Nearly everyone in the office greeted me as I made my way in the door, and I spoke with Debby, Jeannette and David at the front desk. Rich, Paul and Tom Raulli also voiced their concern and support; and I took a deep breath and put on my best happy face. Before I broke away from the scene, Tom asked me to see him in his office.

Just the year before, Tom and our good friend, Robert Rayo, had joined Jeff, me and a half-dozen friends at Yankee Stadium for a Yankees-Mets game. Evidently Jeff had made an impression on Tom.

"Here," Tom said. "Give this to your brother."

Tom handed me a bat that he had received from the Hall of Fame. It was a bat that had been used by former Yankee Wade Boggs, and it commemorated Boggs' 3,000th career hit. I had begged Tom for that bat over the past five years.

"I hope it cheers him up a little. If I catch you with it in your house, I'll beat you to death with it."

I was happy that Tom had made me laugh, because it stopped me from crying in gratitude.

As I drove back toward Buffalo, I called Jim for the latest report from the hospital and he explained that Jeff was still very quiet, but that they would most definitely work on him the next day. I finally turned on the stereo and listened to sports talk radio as the hosts discussed Alex Rodriguez's use of steroids. I wished so much that I knew how Jeff felt about it, but as I drove, I began to imagine his reaction.

"They all cheated," he'd say. "Who cares as long as he hits forty this year?"

My imagined conversation brought one thing to light. I would always know exactly what he thought about a certain subject because we were of the same mind. The sadness overwhelmed me once more, and I cried over the sound of the host on the sports station. Beside me on the seat was the Boggs' bat. I picked it up and held it as I drove. Of course, I was heading straight to the hospital.

Stepping off the elevator I saw Jim standing in the hallway, speaking with Dave White. Jim's face was full of despair.

"What's up?" I asked. I was holding the bat in my right hand.

"Dave's brother isn't doing real well," Jim said.

I shook Dave's hand and offered my condolences. "Maybe he's just having a bad day," I said.

"No," Dave said. "We're trying to make peace with it. He's going to be having dinner with Jesus soon."

Following an extremely awkward pause, I held the bat up for examination. Jim took a couple of practice swings and marveled at the lightness of the bat. "I don't think Jeff will get the full effect," he said. "He's been asleep the entire day."

I shook Dave's hand once more and made the long

walk to ICU room four.

Jeff's eyes were closed. A cough ravaged him and lifted him off the bed.

"Keep fighting, buddy," I whispered.

I thought of my early-morning crude question to God. I felt like shouting it down the halls of the hospital.

The next day brought a whole new feeling of hope. The staff worked to switch Jeff's feeding tube to his stomach, the trach tube was removed and the shunt was inserted in an effort to relieve the pressure of excess fluids. Kathy headed straight to the hospital after work, and I greeted the boys as they stepped off the school bus. It was killing me not to see how Jeff looked immediately following the procedures, but Lynn, Jim and my parents were by his side. Kathy's visit with Jeff went through dinner. Our plan was to just switch places, but Kathy came in and sat down at the kitchen table. Before she could articulate even a single word, she broke down. "He looks so good," she said, her voice ragged with tears. "I couldn't help it, when I saw his face clean-shaven, and when he opened his eyes, I just lost it."

She was losing it again. I hugged her, but the tears kept coming.

"He's just got to be all right," she cried. "There are way too many people who love him."

I thought of poor Dave White. Certainly he loved his brother as much as we loved ours. Sometimes we lose the ones we love.

"He's fighting so hard," Kathy said. Then she repeated something I'd said just a few days before. "This is Jeff we're talking about!"

Later that night I sat in the quiet of Jeff's room. His television was on, but I was the only one watching it. Jeff's clean-shaven face didn't offer me the comfort I needed because he was still far away from me. I glanced around the room, taking in the cards from friends and family. My eyes centered on the homemade card from Johnny, Rocco and Farrah. The card was adorned with smiley faces and a picture of the sun high in the sky. The children, in stilted handwriting, were begging for Jeff to come home.

"That's what I'm talking about, God," I whispered. "That's why I want to know what the hell the plan is here!"

I thought of how happy Jeff had been at the birth of each of his children. I recalled our telephone conversation in the moments immediately following Farrah's birth.

"Farrah?" I asked. "You named her Farrah?"

"Yeah, and she's beautiful," Jeff said.

"Like Farrah Fawcett?"

"Exactly," Jeff answered.

"She'll have to be beautiful to live up to that name," I said.

"Well it's a good thing she is then," Jeff said. "She's my beautiful reward."

As usual Jeff hung up the phone without even a simple good-bye, but this time the hum of the disconnect didn't bother me one bit because the love in his voice continued to echo in my ear.

The announcement of Jeff and Lynn's third child was a bit of a surprise. To be sure, there wasn't a single morning of my adult life when I did not speak to Jeff. It didn't matter where we were, or what was going on, we talked every day. Normally we spoke of the condition of the Yankees' pitching staff, how our football picks worked out, what music we were listening to or how we could arrange it so that we were together over the weekend. A lot of my social plans were finalized during those conversations as I fell in line with whatever party or golf outing or dinner Jeff was planning. Every day of Jeff's life started with some sort of plan as he contemplated the twenty-four hours ahead. That was why I was so surprised when he relayed the latest bit of news. I'd had no idea whatsoever that it was something that he had planned.

"Lynn's pregnant again," he said in one of our early morning conversations.

"Dude, are you out of your mind?" I asked.

I was thrilled for him because I heard the excitement in his voice, but his life was certainly way too busy to add another child to the mix, wasn't it?

"It's awesome," he said. "I can't wait to hold another kid."

I just laughed at him. "Three kids, a dog, a job where you work ten hours a day, and a bad back. Like I said, you're out of your mind." -

"Think about it," Jeff said. "Mom and Dad had six kids. I don't work any harder than they had to. The hell with it! The more the merrier."

"So now you're having six kids?" I asked.

"No! This is it, but it's awesome."

Of course, it took the requisite nine months before Jeff and Lynn's moment of pure love entered the world. Rocco Jeffrey Fazzolari was born on June 27, 2006, at 10:38 p.m. I believe that the news of Rocco's birth reached my ears by about 10:45 that night.

"Congratulations!" I exclaimed.

"He's just perfect," Jeff answered. "We're doing good, aren't we?"

"We're doing great," I answered. "Kiss Lynn for me and tell her thanks."

As usual, the line went dead in my ear.

We didn't have to wait long to meet Rocco. Just two weeks later, Jeff and Lynn hosted a party to mark Farrah's third birthday.

"What is he serving today?" Kathy asked as we made the short drive to Jeff and Lynn's home. "I can't imagine that he had much time to prepare a feast."

I just glanced at my wife. "Are you kidding me?" I asked.

"They just had the baby," Kathy said. "If it were me, I'd just order a couple of pizzas."

There wasn't a single slice of pizza to be found. Jeff had prepared baked chicken, stuffed peppers, a pasta dish in a light marinara sauce, a potato salad, a macaroni salad and three different vegetable dishes. The thirty or forty guests were well stuffed, and there was certainly enough food left over to feed at least twenty more.

As soon as dinner was over, the cars were moved out of the way and we shot baskets in the driveway until late in the evening. Despite the fact that his back was barking, Jeff played each and every game, reveling in the fun.

"Doesn't look like a third kid cramped your style," I said.

"Oh no," he said. "In fact, it made me want to throw the greatest party ever. Did you get enough to eat, pumpkin?"

I couldn't do anything other than marvel at his strength. About an hour after all other guests had left, I watched Jeff lean into the crib to lift Rocco. He cringed with the back movement he'd been forced to make, but a second later, he smiled as he held his son out for my inspection.

"He's already big," I said.

"He's huge!" Jeff said. "Look at the size of his hands. They look like Grandpa Fuzzy's hands."

I touched Rocco's hands.

"I think about the Bruce line in Long Time Coming," Jeff said. "How he talks about his kids and prays that he can just provide a life that is free of all sins that aren't of their own making."

"You'll do it," I said. "You'll get it done."

Jeff lowered Rocco back into the crib.

"Yeah, if it doesn't break my back to lift this kid."

We headed out to the back porch to have another beer

and to toast another resounding milestone in our wonderful lives.

***

The wind was howling. I headed out of the front door of the hospital, and bundled myself against the cold. The clouds were heavy in the sky blocking out the stars and even the moon. When I looked up I saw nothing at all except for the darkness that seemed intent on surrounding me.

"I'm not giving up on You, God," I said.

Then I got into my car and headed home.

The sun rose again the next day. In my frenzied state of mind, I wasn't even sure that would happen. I was overcome by the realization that Jeff's quality of life could be extremely changed. Feeling as if I were on automatic pilot, I headed to the hospital, hoping against hope that Jeff would be more responsive.

Jim and Carrie were there before me. Jeff had been moved out of the ICU and into room five twenty nine, but that was little consolation. The move to the pre-rehab floor should have been considered a step in the right direction, but we had been cautioned by the staff that the move to the lower floor did not mean that Jeff was out of the woods, or that he would return to us as good as new.

"He's going to make a full recovery," Carrie said. "You just watch. He'll stun all of them."

Jeff's eyes were open, but he was staring right through us.

"I do believe he will," I said. "But it's so tiring, isn't it?"

"This is no time to quit," Carrie said. "There hasn't been a Fazzolari made who throws in the towel."

Later that night, after enduring another long day of hope, I sat at the computer and recounted the one scene that had pushed me forward through the trying day at Jeff's bedside. I had needed to write it all down, somewhere, so that I could make some sense of what I was feeling. I wrote quickly, and efficiently, but cried as I did so.

***

"Life is difficult when you're always on; always appreciating what you should appreciate. Living in crisis mode makes if extremely difficult to always be there and with it. It's the reason why The Brady Bunch, Deal or No Deal, and Gilligan's Island are popular. We all need to put our brains in low gear from time to time.

"So I was really scuffling when I returned to Jeff's bedside today. The only saving grace was that it was Saturday and a couple of my siblings would be there for Jeff. Carrie and Jim joined me for the early morning shift with Corinne and John scheduled to join us a little later. In the middle of it all there was a moment...a big moment.

"Carrie and I stood on either side of the bed. Jeff's eyes darted back and forth as we spoke to him, and softly, without warning, Carrie reached out and touched Jeff's left cheek.

"The moment was absolutely perfect as Jeff seemed to lean into Carrie's touch, and she moved her hand and caressed Jeff's face in such a loving manner that all of life seemed to stop. I no longer heard the sounds of the hospital room. I could no longer hear the alarm for his IV, a sound that drove me absolutely crazy, just seconds before. I could no longer smell the hospital smells. I could not sense the traffic moving by on the street below his room.

"Instead, I concentrated on Carrie's soothing hand and Jeff's response. Slowly Carrie traced his face, touching his eyebrows, outlining his features and smiling broadly as she did so. Jeff was smiling right along with her. I just knew that he was and I became entranced in the moment.

"I thought of all of Jeff and Carrie's special moments together; not my moments with Jeff, but simply her wonderful moments with her big brother. As kids, they applied make-up to each other. There were many times Jeff made Carrie laugh so hard that the beverage she was drinking came out of her nose.

"Each moment raced through my mind, all in a split second that was now standing still.

"I watched for as long as I could and then I turned away as tears gathered in my eyes.

"That's all the beauty I can take," I said, stealing a line from a Springsteen song.

"What's that?" Carrie asked, oblivious to the waves of emotion threatening to break to the shore of my emotional wellbeing.

"Nothing," I choked back.

"Just when I thought I was sick of being on the edge, just when I thought I was at the virtual breaking point, pure and simple love sent me surging ahead. It was a complete, unconditional love, presented in a simple touch.

"Thanks Jeff. Thanks Carrie. Thank you, God, for letting me see it."

Chapter XI – What Love Can Do

February 23-February 28, 2009   Live as if you were to die tomorrow. Learn as if you were to live forever.   Mahatma Gandhi.

The family was absolutely reeling by the end of the weekend, and I felt powerless to help anyone. It was all that I could do to struggle out of bed and face another day of despair. Yet I had to try. For Jeff's sake and for the sake of everyone else who was sucking it up and toughing it out, I had to make the effort.

I rolled out of bed at 4:30a.m. Monday and rushed through the usual preparations. I was on the road to the hospital by 5:15 a.m. My telephone message alert sounded as soon as I sat down in the car. I listened to the replay of a message that Jim had left in the middle of the night.

"I might not make it into the hospital in the morning. I've been up all night, sick as a dog, and my foot is the size of your head. I got the gout, bad!"

My mind was kicked into a frenzied state. I needed to be at work by 8 a.m. if Jim couldn't make it, who would handle the morning shift?

I thought about saying a quick prayer, but I was still having severe doubts about whether or not God was listening. Instead, I jumped from the car and hustled up the ramp to the hospital. I stepped into the slow-moving elevator, with a cup of coffee spilling over the brim and onto my hand. A nurse and a doctor shared the ride with me.

"Good morning," the nurse said as the door closed.

"How are you?" I asked.

"Tired," she said. "For some reason I didn't want to get out of bed this morning."

I had no intention of continuing the small talk. I didn't need to hear about why her life was so tough. The doctor punched the button for the seventh floor, and I asked him to hit five for me.

The elevator started, lurched, ground a little and then stopped completely.

"What the hell was that?" I asked.

"Oh, we're stuck between floors," the nurse said. "This happened to me once before." She was dressed in white right down to the shoes. The giddiness in her voice was getting a little irritating. She hit the emergency button, and a voice came to us over the speakers.

"Just stay in the car," the man said. "We'll have you out in no time."

If I were alone in that car, I might have punched the wall. Instead, I stared at the floor in absolute silence.

"Think of it this way," the cheerful nurse said. "Now we can relax our minds and take control of our days. The maintenance guys will free us, and we'll be perfectly refreshed."

"Unless," I said, "the elevator plummets four floors and obliterates us all."

The doctor chuckled, but the nurse reacted as if I'd shot her. "My God!" she said, "why would you say something like that?"

"Because that's exactly how my year has been going so far."

We waited for about twenty minutes. We didn't say another word to one another, and I didn't give two shits about it.

By 8 a.m. two things were abundantly clear. First and foremost, Jeff was still sleeping soundly with little chance of waking up and talking, and secondly, Jim wasn't going to be able to get to the hospital in time so that I could do my job. It really didn't matter to me all that much, but in my state of mind, it was turning into an emergency. I didn't have to hold on much longer, though, because John and my father arrived at just about the same time.

"Is he doing any better?" Dad asked. I saw the hopefulness in my father's eyes, but he quickly noted the despair in mine. "Well I'm here now. Go do what you need to do."

I stopped by Jeff's bed once more. I took my brother's hand and asked for a squeeze. I didn't get any response at all.

"Keep resting, pal. They're going to work you a little today."

I brought my hand to Jeff's face and touched his right cheek. All at once he began coughing, and the violence of the spasms lifted him off the bed. I ran from the room. I just couldn't see any more that morning.

During the course of the day I couldn't help but run memories in my mind. Chuck called me early in the morning, and once more I marveled at his timing. It was as if he had a beeper that alerted him when I was at my wit's end. He assured me that he and Corinne would take a seat at the foot of Jeff's bed. Chuck provided another pep talk that lifted my spirits. The other thing that he did was to provide me with a vivid recollection of a truly wonderful day.

"You know what I was just thinking about?" Chuck asked.

"What's that?"

"When we bought you dinner at Red Lobster.

I started laughing.

"Think about that as you work today," Chuck said. "It'll bring a smile to your face."

As I made my way through my workday, the entire story unfolded in my mind's eye.

The telephone rang early on Saturday morning in 1988. I was in the middle of doing a final edit on my second book, Eye in the Sky. I wasn't in much of a hurry to answer the phone, so I allowed the machine to grab it.

"What's up, Moe?" Jeff asked. He was shouting into the phone. "You aren't sleeping, are you? Come on, fatty... get the phone. Come on, you can do it...just a little further. Come on! Pretend it's a doughnut."

"What?" I asked as I finally grabbed the phone.

"I hope I didn't wake you," Jeff said.

"No, I'm working on the book," I said.

"Fabulous. It's just stupendous, actually. How's it going? I'm worried about you."

"Jeff, what do you want?"

"I was just saying good morning."

"Good morning," I said with a trace of bitterness in my voice.

"Ah, don't be like that," Jeff said. "Now you're going to feel bad after I tell you why I'm calling."

"What do you want?" I shouted.

"Chuckie and I have decided to meet you for lunch," he said. "We're talking Red Lobster."

"I can't go," I said. "The book has to be to the publisher on Monday morning."

"That's why we're taking you. It's a celebration of your accomplishment. We'll see you at noon."

"I can't go!" I yelled, but I was talking to the dial tone as Jeff had already hung up.

I was living alone in a small four-room apartment about five miles outside of the city of Buffalo. Jeff was obviously looking for something to do and I hoped he'd respect that I needed to work. I quickly forgot the call as I went back to work on the final edit. There was a new urgency to my work, however, because despite my objections, in the back of my mind I knew that he'd still come to the door with Chuck in tow.

At a few minutes before noon there was a loud staccato knock on the window of my office/bedroom. The startling knock nearly caused me to jump clear of my skin, and about thirty consecutive rings of the doorbell followed. I opened the door to my two smiling guests, and Jeff thrust a Budweiser in my direction.

"No way," I said. "I'll go to lunch, but I'm not drinking anything. I have too much work to do."

"Ah, don't be difficult," Jeff said. "This party is in your honor."

I nodded in Chuck's direction, and he smiled as if to say that it was pointless to resist. I grabbed the beer.

"Chug it down," Jeff said. "I'm starving. I'm going to eat a five-pound lobster."

I turned the cap on the beer. I locked eyes with Jeff, hoping to talk a little sense into him before we headed to the restaurant. "I'll have a couple of beers and lunch, but I have to be back here in an hour. Do you understand that?"

"Sixty minutes. I got it."

I drank the beer as we stood in the parking lot and talked.

"It's a glorious day, isn't it?" he asked. "We should go golfing."

"Dude…" I started.

"Yeah, yeah, you have an hour! Let's go."

Within minutes we were seated at a table at Red Lobster. The meal began with shrimp cocktail and a platter of fried shrimp, followed by a dozen raw clams that we shared. Chuck and Jeff each ordered a Bloody Mary as I nursed a beer and glanced at the clock.

"Please, just relax," Jeff said. "We're trying to do something nice for you here and you're like a bag of nerves. Tell us about the story you're working on."

I had just about enough. Instead of answering him, I headed to the restroom. When I returned there were shots of tequila all around.

"What're you doing?" I asked.

"When you were gone, we got to talking," Jeff said. "Charles and I feel that you don't take the time to enjoy your accomplishments. We're ready to force you to do so. Would you like salt and lemon with that shot?"

I glanced at Chuck. He was usually the sensible one. Today, he was simply along for the ride. He raised his shot glass.

Jeff offered a truly disgusting toast and we tossed back the shot.

"That tasted like it needs another one," Jeff said. "By the way, we took the liberty of ordering for you while you visited the restroom. We're all getting double lobster tails."

"You know how much this lunch is going to cost you?" I asked.

"Money is no object," Jeff answered. "We're just so proud of you."

The one-hour lunch stretched into a two-and-a-half hour ordeal. We not only had a second shot of tequila, we had a third, fourth and fifth too. Editing the book would have to wait until Sunday morning when I would have to do it with a full hangover.

I was absolutely stuffed when the pretty waitress returned to the table carrying our check. She handed it to Jeff and he took it without hesitation. He studied it for a long while and then shoved it across the table to Chuck who also eyeballed it for some time.

"Is there a problem?" the waitress asked.

"Yeah, what do you do if people eat and then don't have enough money to pay?" Jeff asked.

The young waitress took a step back and offered a

172

nervous smile. "I guess we'd have to call the cops," she said.

"Well, you better get them on the line," Jeff said, "because Chuck and I didn't bring a dime, and we really don't want to stiff Cliff with the bill."

Once more I looked to Chuck for even a hint of cooperation.

"I didn't even bring my wallet," Chuck said.

The waitress looked my way.

"Come on!" I said. "You have money, right?" I asked Jeff.

"Sorry, buddy, this one's on you," Jeff said. "It was all your idea, wasn't it, Chuck?"

"That's how I see it," Chuck said.

I actually made Jeff and Chuck stand up and empty their pockets. The sons-of-bitches couldn't have made change for a quarter. This was actually happening. Finally, I slid my American Express to the waitress.

Jeff's face broke into a wide grin. "Oh, miss," he said. "Can you add three more shots of tequila to that tab?"

The poor girl looked to me for approval.

"Whatever," I said.

"That's my boy," Jeff said. "Enjoy life! We're just so proud of you!"

The celebratory lunch cost me $240.

Before we left the restaurant, Jeff put an arm around my shoulder.

"Say, do you remember that time when you and Mom stiffed me out of breakfast after church?"

"You waited this long to pay me back?" I asked.

"Laugh it up," Jeff said.

***

Despite the wonderful memory, my mind was a jumbled mess as I struggled through my workday. I spoke with each one of my siblings, Lynn and my parents about the exhaustive rehabilitation that Jeff faced. As the day went along, Lynn called each of us to explain that the healthcare staff would meet with us, as a family, to discuss Jeff's continued care. We had been informed that the rehab work would outlast Jeff's medical insurance and that long-term care was extremely expensive.

"We'll all mortgage our homes again if we have to," I told Lynn. "Whatever it takes."

Yet the horror of the situation hung over all of us. Where would Jeff's rehab work take place? Could we possibly get him into the best place? What were they talking about when they mentioned acute or sub-acute care?

As far as I was concerned, every question had the same answer. It was all about love. For each and every day that my brother spent walking the earth there was an ache in my heart. I loved him so much that the ache often times presented itself as worry about him. Yet there were moments when the ache was simply pride in how he was living his life. Often that ache took the form of sharp pains caused by laughing along with him. Yet we always stood, shoulder to shoulder and side by side, partners in life, always keenly aware that we shared some sort of secret on living the right way. We knew and loved the Yankees and Springsteen. We were certain that we'd never be wrong on those two constants.

We also understood that we were never to turn our backs on our family members. We played defense for each other, knowing that life could sometimes get in the way, believing that we were on a clean and certain path. We understood that God was lighting our way, but we also felt as if we had the inside scoop on what was right and wrong. Perhaps we didn't have much insight into the mysterious ways of the universe, but we tried to live life the right way. That is one thing that I'm sure of.

Yet Jeff wasn't available to me right now. I was so

used to going to him for some sort of answer that this difficult time was even more troublesome. I didn't have my main ally helping me through!

"It's ridiculous!" I screamed as I drove through the city of Buffalo heading to my next job.

Oh God! I thought, Jeff and I are supposed to ride this out together, laughing all the way. We are supposed to be side by side, trading advice, enjoying each other's successes and basking in the success of our children. But Jeff wasn't with me now. The ache of love that was the mere presence of him in my heart was now an ache so raw and unforgiving that it felt like an open wound that was horribly infected.

But we would handle the rehab. There would come a day when I would be able to talk with Jeff and share my life with him. Jeff was dealt a bum hand, but he would be back beside me, driving the cart of our love to the very edge of the horizon, jumping off and laughing as the non-essential supplies tumbled over the precipice.

He held an ache in his heart for me and countless others as well. Yet the space in his heart where love was saved was much more expansive. It was space that could carry a sign that read, 'Open All Night. We Never Close.'

As the day went along, my mind continued to replay day after day of the life that I had shared with my brother and best buddy. I recalled one day in particular when I was so proud of him that I thought my heart would explode.

In 1987, for the first time in many years, the North Collins Eagles varsity basketball team was causing a bit of excitement in the small town. Former standout player Chris Heinold, who had starred on the Canisius College team just the year before, coached the team. Jeff was the best player on the team, averaging nearly sixteen points per game.

I drove Jeff to the big game at the North Collins gym. The team needed a win against the heavily favored Springville team.

"You need to look for your shot more," I said. "I've seen every game you've played this year, and the best chance you guys have of winning is for you to have a big game."

"I'll get my shots," Jeff said. "But I can't just gun. There are other guys on the team."

"Look for your shot first," I said. "In fact, if you score twenty tonight, I'll give you twenty bucks."

Jeff took a long, hard, contemplative look at me. "Ah, you want to make it interesting, huh? How about twenty bucks for twenty points and five bucks for every point over twenty?"

I would have agreed to anything to get him to shoot more. "You got it," I said.

I settled into my seat just behind the team's bench to watch Jeff warm up. He looked a little nervous in the pre-game warm-ups, and I swear he didn't even make a single shot. As he stepped off the court just before the introductions, he glanced at me.

"I hope you stopped at the bank," he said.

The first half of the game was a blur of long three-pointers and stolen passes. By my count, Jeff had seventeen of the team's first twenty-five points. He was taking a shot every single time he got free and most of them were tickling the bottom of the net. He never even glanced in my direction, as the score was tight and Coach Heinold had the team's undivided attention. How much was this going to cost me?

The second half started with Jeff drilling a three-pointer from deep in the corner to secure the twenty dollars. My heart was full of pride, but the proud feelings soon turned to laughter as he made his way up the court. In the middle of his scramble to get back on defense, he turned to find me in the crowd. He raised his right hand and pointed in my direction. He knew exactly how many points he had!

After the game, I pulled the car around by the locker room door. North Collins had lost by one as the final play of the game saw an errant pass sail over Jeff's head. He had been wide open and would have certainly buried that last-second shot.

Jeff tossed his gym bag into the backseat.

"Can you believe that last play?" he asked.

"Yeah, it was rough," I said. "You probably aren't even worried about how many points you scored." I was trying to distract him, hoping that he'd let me slide on the money I owed him.

"Dude," he said, "let's not be silly. I scored thirty-one. That'll be seventy-five-clams please."

It was the best seventy-five dollars I ever spent.

Later in the year, the family was invited back to a game for the annual Class Night event. In a tribute to the parents, the school invited all of the mothers onto the court to be introduced with their sons. Jeff was understandably proud to share the moment with Mom, and he stood in line with a flower that he was going to pin to Mom and deliver with a kiss. What Jeff didn't know was that Mom had her own prank planned. "Jeff Fazzolari and his mother Lynda," the announcer called over the loud speaker.

Jeff walked onto the court and Mom entered wearing a wig and a clown nose.

"What're you doing?" Jeff asked as the crowd roared.

"You're always doing it to everyone else," Mom said. "I'm finally getting you back."

There is a lovely photo of the incident; Jeff wore a sheepish smile as he pinned the flower on Mom, who was laughing so hard and was so proud.

That night I returned home to see Jake, Matt and Sam

playing a video game together. I thought of all the games I'd shared with my brothers, and I stood in the doorway listening to their playful banter.

"Do you have to go to the hospital again tonight?" Sam asked. I could tell by the look in his eyes that he wanted me to stick around for a while.

"I have to," I said. "You know that, right?"

"But Uncle Jeff will be home soon?"

"Yeah, pretty soon," I said. "But even if it takes a long time I have to help him, okay?"

"Okay," Sam said.

Matt and Jake were growing impatient with the conversation, but only because they wanted Sam back in the game.

"Play with your brothers," I said.

Twenty minutes later, as I headed back to the hospital, one of those moments that I had shared with my brothers came crashing into my skull and stuck there.

Dad was always ready with a long list of chores for us on every weekend morning. All four boys were expected to be ready to plant the garden, weed the garden, or pick the vegetables, and such a day usually began by 7 a.m. at the latest. It was clearly a much-hated activity that led to a few sour faces as the work began.

One such morning will forever live in the memory banks of all who were there. Dad had bellowed his way through the house, shaking us all from slumber, as it was time to clear the garden of rocks and till the soil. Now we aren't talking about a small plot of land here. The normal garden consisted of about a hundred tomato plants, pepper plants, lettuce, potatoes, zucchini, beans, squash... nearly every vegetable imaginable. So, on that morning, the land that needed to be cleared would cost us most of the day.

We headed off to our living hell with the instruction to

pick up each and every rock and throw it in the direction of the woods so that Dad could work the tiller and not hit a rock every few seconds.

"This sucks," John announced as we all got started.

"We can't revolt," I mentioned. I was so tired that I could barely keep my eyes open.

Jeff and Jim took one area of the garden as John and I cleared the other. Dad worked the tiller right up the center. Rock after rock flew across the garden and disappeared into the weeds on the other side. Of course, we tried to make a game of it, seeing who could toss their rock the furthest, but it was all about the one rock that never made it to the weeds.

Jim and Jeff, mimicking John's efforts to sail the rocks as far as he could, were rearing back and really hurling them over my father's head and into the weeds. One of the rocks that Jim rifled didn't quite make it. We all watched in horror as the rock struck my father in the center of the forehead. The tiller was still lurching forward when Dad dropped to one knee, and it looked as if a pistol blast had signaled the start of a race. All four boys went screaming out of the garden at a breakneck pace in an effort to get clear before he was on his feet again.

Thankfully Dad was okay, but even some thirty years later the story would always start with, "Remember when we were clearing rocks..." and we would all laugh along.

When I arrived at Jeff's beside on the morning of February 26 there was a wide range of things that I was rooting for. Of course, I wanted desperately to see Jeff a bit more alert, but there was also a selfish side to my agenda. I didn't want to see any more coverage on the airplane disaster, as the pain of what the families of those victims were experiencing was too much to handle. Also, there was one particular nurse who I didn't want to see working on Jeff. He always seemed preoccupied with everything but doing his job the right way, and I didn't feel like making small talk with him as Jeff lay in that bed.

The lights were off in room five twenty nine so I entered slowly. I glanced at the dry-erase board and saw the night nurse's name written there. It wasn't the guy who drove me crazy, so at least I had that going for me. Slowly, I made my way around the bed to the side where Jeff's head was turned. It was almost as if he had positioned himself to look out the window.

I negotiated my way around the bed before I finally glanced down to see that Jeff's eyes were wide open. "Hey there, pumpkin," I said.

(Through the years, Jeff had referred to me as his pumpkin oh, let's say, a million times).

His eyes were looking right through me. There were beads of sweat on his forehead, and his left leg seemed to be in some sort of spasm.

I softly touched the side of Jeff's face, and he blinked under the touch.

"I'm so sorry you're going through this," I whispered. "It's still just a time-out though. They're going to start working with you and exercising you. It'll be okay."

I followed Jeff's eyes to the side window and the rising sun. I wondered if he could understand that another day was about to begin and that he was one day closer to getting out of the bed. He closed his eyes.

I sat in the chair beside the bed for a couple of hours as Jeff slept peacefully. During those minutes I read the notebook to understand what Corinne had been through during the evening hour stretch, and I was once more in awe of her strength. Corinne had exercised with Jeff for hours, lifting his right arm, left leg, left arm and then right leg. She was smart enough to understand that he needed to start to move, even if the hospital staff seemed intent on leaving Jeff immobile until they pushed him out the door.

I finally arrived at the train of thought that had been tormenting me. Why were we suddenly alone in this battle? Why did it seem that the staff had sort of abandoned the case, leaving Lynn and Corinne scrambling to find a rehab facility? For the first two hours of my stay, not a single nurse had even stopped by. What the hell was going on?

Almost as if someone had heard the thoughts in my head, a man with a stethoscope entered the room behind me. "How's Jeff this morning?" he asked.

His simple question had nearly caused me to jump out of my skin.

"I'm sorry for startling you," he said. He introduced himself as a member of the neurological team. He was a short, lean man with a firm handshake.

"I was just surprised to see anyone here," I said. "He's been sweating as he sleeps, coughing hard enough to lift him out of the bed and having leg spasms. I rang the nurse, but here I sit."

The doctor sighed heavily. "I can understand your frustration," he said. "This is a very disturbing injury, and when you feel as if you aren't getting the attention you deserve, it becomes aggravating."

Together we headed to the bed. The doctor took his time in examining Jeff, and for good measure, he wiped some of the sweat from Jeff's brow. "The sweating is caused by temperature changes in the body as Jeff's brain repairs and tries to regulate itself. The cool wash rags provide some relief."

I smiled as I recalled something that Chuck had written in the notebook.

"My brother Jim thought of the washrag," I said. "He said that he saw it on an episode of Bonanza. The father put the washrag on Little Joe's head and in a matter of no time, Little Joe was up eating stew."

The doctor laughed. "I wish it were that easy," he said. "But please know that Jeff has been progressing. Unfortunately, it takes a long time to battle through this."

"So he'll be all right?" I asked.

"He has to keep progressing," the doctor said.

It wasn't exactly the ringing endorsement I was looking for, but it did calm me. I shook hands again with the doctor and thanked him for coming by. Before settling back into my chair beside the bed, I called Lynn's cell phone number, but it went straight to voicemail. I couldn't imagine all that she was going through trying to hold it all together. As difficult as it was for me, it had to be so much worse for her as she tried to put on a brave face for the children. Without a lot of coaxing, I shifted back in time to Jeff and Lynn's wedding day.

***

The wedding of Jeff Fazzolari and Lynn Karm was highly anticipated and certainly well attended. Family and friends gathered at Holy Spirit Church in North Collins for the ceremony that brought tears to the eyes of those in attendance, as weddings will often do. The tears in the eyes of those gathered at the back of the church were tears of sadness as well as happiness. Just a few days earlier, one of our great friends, Jeff Renaldo, had been injured in a work-related accident, and although he was in the hospital, he was certainly with us in spirit. Thankfully, Jeff Renaldo was able to join in the celebration just a few weeks later.

The back vestibule of the church was a bustle of activity. Jeff's best man, Mike Livecchi, brothers Jim, John and Cliff and the rest of his groomsmen surrounded Jeff. There may have been a pre-wedding beer or two involved. In fact, I toasted Jeff just moments before the ceremony began.

"Are you ready for this, brother?" I asked.

"I love her a lot," Jeff said in a moment of true sincerity. He offered up a Bruce quote from the song Brilliant Disguise.

"Bruce got divorced after that album came out," I said, and we laughed.

Jeff, of course, was ready to play the very first joke on his new bride. Unbeknownst to anyone, Jeff had decorated the bottom of his own shoes with the words, "Help Me." When he knelt down next to his beautiful bride, everyone in the first few rows shared a laugh. Yet the comical aspect of the day was just beginning.

Arriving at the reception hall at the beautiful Como Restaurant in Niagara Falls, each guest was handed a pair of plastic sunglasses and a Hawaiian lei. I recall passing Lynn on the stairs and giving her a quizzical look.

"We're married!" she said as she hugged me. "We're here for a party."

The food was unbelievable, of course. One of the reasons why the reception was held in Niagara Falls was so The Como Restaurant could prepare the food. Jeff and Lynn wanted to share a perfect meal with the people they loved. They made it even "more perfect" as Jeff prepared the Italian sausage that was served that night. The Italian desserts were homemade, courtesy of the hard-working mother of the groom.

As the guests entered the reception hall there was an additional surprise. An absolutely stunning ice sculpture depicting a bride and groom was placed front and center.

"Who did that?" I asked Jeff.

"My work partner Tim Bucko and me," Jeff said.

"Where'd you learn how to do that?" I asked in amazement.

"I told you that was what I was studying," Jeff said. "Dude, I have talents you can't even imagine."

I was so proud of him and so thrilled for him that I couldn't stop myself from giving him a strong hug.

"Get off me," he said laughing.

Every time I walked through the front entrance, I stared at that ice sculpture. It was more than a little amazing to me. I imagined his hand working to craft the perfect model before me. After downing about six pieces of Italian sausage, I realized that Jeff was more an artist than a chef.

About halfway through the ceremony, Jeff summoned me to his side. "It's time for Thunder Road," he said. "Raise Lynn in the chair. She knows all about it."

A few years earlier, on the advice of a good friend, Mike Palmer, we had started a ritual that included lifting the bride high in a chair as Springsteen's Thunder Road played over the speakers. To Lynn's credit, she was unbelievably prepared for the event. We held her high, serenading her with our best Bruce impressions. We changed the last line to suit the occasion.

"So Lynn, climb in, it's a town full of losers and we're pulling out of here to win."

I remember that, following the song, Jeff grabbed each of his siblings in a hug of celebration. The front of his shirt was soaked with sweat, and the sunglasses that he wore through the entire ceremony were askew as he gripped us tightly.

"My blood brothers and sisters! Thank you! I love you!"

"We both love you all," I responded, remembering what he had mistakenly said at John and Dana's wedding.

On that morning the next visitor to the hospital room was actually a welcome face. Frank Guido was still making visits to Jeff's bedside on a regular basis, and his terrific sense of humor was something that I'd begun to rely on.

"Hey, Clifford," Frank said as he entered the room.

"Where's your brother Jim? Does he still have the gout?"

"Yeah, he's hurting," I said.

Frank snapped on a pair of gloves and approached the bedside. In mid-sentence, he cleared Jeff's congestion. "I don't feel sorry for Jim," Frank said. "He sits there telling me how much his foot hurts and then he heads down to the cafeteria and fills his face with bologna sandwiches and sausages. He's a freaking pig."

Suddenly I was laughing. Frank touched Jeff's forehead, removed the washcloth and tossed it in the direction of the laundry bin.

"Clifford!" he yelled out. "What a horrible name that is. Clifford!"

I knew that Frank was just trying to cheer me up by making fun of my name, and it was working.

Frank headed to the bathroom. He took his time in preparing another cool washcloth as I sat in the chair laughing.

"Did your mother lose a bet? Is that why she named you Clifford?"

Frank returned to the bed, gently placed the blue cloth on Jeff's head, and touched my brother's right cheek. "Come on, Jeff, you have to get out of that bed. Your brothers are some real assholes."

Frank saluted me and headed back out the door, leaving my laughter in his wake. I couldn't help but think of how much Jeff would enjoy a man like Frank.

As Frank exited the room, I considered another celebration when Jeff's sense of humor won, at my expense.

In 1995, the Christmas celebration was in full swing. For the first time my girlfriend Kathy was joining the party, and two steps in past the door Jeff hit her with a smart-ass comment about how goofy her hair looked.

"I'm thinking we have a drink," he said to me. "At school I learned the best Bloody Mary recipe. You in?"

"I'm in," I answered.

The drink was in my hand just a few minutes after I took off my coat. There was a huge stalk of celery sticking out of the glass, which looked more like a meal than a drink.

"Try it," Jeff said.

Over the years I had tried a number of Bloody Marys; how much better could it be? Yet one sip in, I knew he was studying well at school. There was a good bite to it; he must have used a full bottle of hot sauce. "Nice!" I said.

"Sip it, though, you don't have to gun it down like Otis." (He was referring to the town drunk on the Andy Griffith Show).

So I sipped the drink. We were only at my parents home for a short visit anyway, as we had another party to attend at Kathy's sister's home.

"One more," Jeff said when my glass was finally empty.

I hadn't wanted to drink much, but the drink had been so good. I handed my glass over. "Go easy." I said, "For some reason that one got me a little dizzy. Must be that I didn't eat much."

"That has to be it," he said with a smile.

The second Bloody Mary tasted even better, but Kathy was ready to go, and rather than simply sip it, I drank it down quickly, kissed my parents good-bye and shook Jeff's hand on the way out the door.

"Good drinks," I said.

He laughed.

"Why is he laughing?" Kathy asked.

"Who knows?" I said.

Twenty minutes later, I knew. I was so drunk that every word out of my mouth was a slur, and each movement of my head seemed to take an hour.

"What happened to you?" Kathy asked. The expression on her face was a cross between worry and amusement.

I dialed my parents' home. "Where's Jeff?" I choked out.

"Right here, he's making the gravy," my mother said.

"Put that idiot on the phone," I slurred.

"You sound drunk," my mother said.

"Yeah, well, where's Jeff?"

"Yellow!" Jeff yelled. "Too much drinky-poo?" he asked.

"What did you do?" I asked. "How much vodka did I drink?"

"About half a bottle," he said. "The school taught us to mix them so that you can't even taste the alcohol. Have a good time at the in-laws."

Jeff hung up before I even had the chance to answer. Kathy glanced at me as she drove. "You have to pace yourself with the drinking," she said.

"Yeah, thanks for the advice," I said.

Christmas with Lorie and Mike and the rest of Kathy's family was pretty much a mess, as all I wanted to do was pass out on the host's couch. Jeff had struck again.

Back in the hospital room, before I even had the chance to settle down from Frank's quick visit, Jeff had another concerned visitor. Carolyn, the ICU nurse who had given her all in the first few days of Jeff's hospitalization, visited the fifth floor. She stood at the foot of the bed with tears in her eyes, just saying over and over again that Jeff would be fine. "He's so loved," she said. "God will take care of him. I'm sure he will be okay."

As I hugged Carolyn and thanked her for checking in on her special patient I couldn't help but think that she was a woman with a truly golden heart.

When Carolyn left, I took my place at Jeff's side. His eyes were open, but he was looking right through me.

"That woman has a golden heart," I said. "Do you remember when you bought that golden heart for Lynn?"

Jeff's eyes closed as if the memory were too hard to handle.

"Sorry about that," I said. "By the way, you were right. Lynn has a golden heart."

In the summer following Johnny's birth Jeff presented Lynn with a huge pendant on a gold chain. The pendant was heart-shaped and was a gift that was prompted by a song by Mark Knopfler, Golden Heart. Jeff showed me the pendant before he presented it to his wife. It was an exact match to the pendant on the cover of the CD-case.

"It's awesome, isn't it?" he asked.

"I suppose," I said. "It's a little big, though, isn't it?"

Jeff shrugged. "I just love the song. I swear watching Lynn have the children just does something to me. Golden heart, man. She has a golden heart."

Later that night, we were all together at a bar, sharing drinks and laughs. Corinne and Chuck, John and Dana, Jim and Lisa, Kathy and I were all there, and the mood was jovial. Lynn wore the golden heart proudly around her neck, and in the middle of the crowded bar, I turned to her. "How'd you win your gold medal?" I asked.

I got the huge laugh that I was gunning for, but for the very first time, I actually saw a hint of true hurt in Jeff's eyes.

"I'm just joking," I said.

"I don't care," Jeff said. "She has a golden heart."

Thinking back on it, going for the joke on a night when Jeff was so proud of all he had in his life was a huge regret. Through all the years, it may have been the only time when I noticed that he was disappointed in something I'd said.

Just before 10 a.m. the family assembled in the hall-way near a conference room on the fifth floor. The team of people involved in Jeff's care had called for the meeting to fill us in on the future treatment plan. It was an essential meeting and one that we had all dreaded attending, but as a group we needed to get back on the same page. Corinne and Lynn were well prepared with notebooks, medical books and a list of questions. My job was to take the minutes of the meeting and make sure that we had it all down for future reference. Jim and Lisa, John and Dad were there to ensure that no stone was left unturned and to provide capable and insightful support.

The wind was quickly let out of our sails as one of Jeff's nurses explained that there was a high likelihood that Jeff would never return to work again, as he most likely would battle poor balance issues and many, many more medical issues.

The reality of it struck each one of us like a hammer to the forehead. How would Jeff respond to such a life? He was a man who took care of the needs of so many others. How would he feel being the one who needed help?

Jeff's nurse told us, once more, about the devastation of the injury. She carefully explained that Jeff needed extensive rehabilitation work, and that Mercy Hospital was not a facility that was capable of such care. She explained that there were a number of excellent acute and sub-acute facilities in the area that excelled in rehabilitation, but that we would need to do the legwork to get Jeff into one of the beds.

"Is it about money?" Dad asked. "Because we'll find the money somehow."

Once more I saw absolute heartbreak in my father's eyes. Suddenly the room became a dizzying space of complete despair. The nurse assured all of us that getting Jeff into the rehab facility of choice wasn't a matter of money, but that the rehab work would be extremely expensive, as it could take longer than a year.

Thankfully, Corinne and Lynn were well prepared, because if the meeting had been left to me, or Jim, or John, it would have ground to a halt. It didn't seem as if any of us could find our voice. The air in the room seemed way too heavy, and the voices of all those who took turns speaking seemed slowed down in some manner. All that we feared was being dumped at our feet, and frankly, jammed down our throats. There was too much anger, too much hurt and too little understanding.

For a long time the question of "why" was once again debated. Why did a healthy man with so much to live for suffer such a fate? Together and alone we all needed a place to put the blame. It was counter-productive to our efforts, but we were angry. The staff did not have an answer for us on the day that Jeff suffered the stroke, and they were no closer to an answer nearly a month later.

"We may never know," Jeff's doctor admitted.

Together Corinne and Lynn asked pointed question after pointed question. Despite the fact that I was keeping the notes, much of what was being said was lost in the confusing space between horror and grief.

Gradually, the meeting progressed as to whether or not it would be prudent to bring the kids to the hospital. Lynn had requested the chance to bring Johnny, Farrah and Rocco to see their Dad, and in the end the doctor explained that there was no bad answer. The doctor calmed our fears by saying that Jeff was medically able to handle such a visit.

As the discussion of the rehab facilities evolved, Corinne mentioned the Erie County Medical Center and its acute rehab program. Jim explained that Frank Guido had talked of a rehab facility in Erie, Pennsylvania, and it was mentioned that lifelong family friend Janice Bantle was also working on gathering information.

I took a couple of real deep breaths as I tried to process it all, but one question still hung in the air. Jim was finally able to piece together the words to ask it. "We've heard it mentioned that Jeff's life expectancy is now one year to ten years. Is that true?"

The doctor took his time in answering the question, but what came out of his mouth was every bit as devastating as a Mike Tyson uppercut. "If Jeff doesn't improve, he's certainly at risk. Given the fact that he's been bed-ridden for so long, and that he still has the trach, he may face additional problems. The other shoe can drop. The brain injury may affect everything else. The better he does, day to day, the more time he will have to recover."

By the time the doctor finished his remarks, everyone at the table was crying.

"Well, we'll see what love can do," John said. "We have a strong family, a lot of prayers and real hope."

The doctor was reflective. "Hope and determination is certainly helpful," he said, "but it may not be all that is necessary for Jeff to get his strength back."

An hour and a half after the meeting started, it was over. If it were about love as we all imagined it to be, Jeff would have been standing among us, hugging, crying and sharing. For God's sake, he would have been there loving his wife, and children, his mother and father and his sisters and brothers. Love wasn't all that was necessary, but we would get back to work to find out what was.

I didn't know about anyone else, but the meeting was absolute torture. As I pulled my coat around me I thought about one more discussion that I'd had with Jeff as we drove to the wake of lifelong family friend Albert DeCarlo.

"I've been right all along," he had said from his spot in the passenger seat. "It's always been about love and family."

"You developed that theory?" I asked.

"I just feel bad for Al, Duke and Tracy," he said. "They got cheated out of all that time with their Dad."

"You go when you're called," I said.

"Thy will be done," Jeff said.

Driving down the street away from the hospital, in the middle of a heavy rain, I allowed the tears to fall. "Thy will be done, but your will has to be my will this time!" I shouted.

Chapter XII – Happy

February 28-March 1, 2009   I tell you the truth, you will
weep and mourn while the world rejoices. You will grieve,
but your grief will turn to joy. John 16:20

On the morning of February 28th I headed to the
hospital for the morning shift with a heart so heavy that I
thought I'd need a wheelbarrow to carry it. It wasn't like
I'd been sleeping for the past three weeks, I knew that
Jeff wasn't making a lot of progress, but to have the staff
frame it for us at the meeting was discouraging. I needed
to find some hope, somewhere.

I headed straight for Jeff's room. The nurses, all
dressed in light blue, were all gathered behind the desk
at the center of the floor and someone said "Good morn-
ing," but I had no idea who it was. Nonetheless, I mut-
tered a greeting.

Jeff was asleep, of course, and the sense of frustration
only continued to grow. I plopped into the chair beside
the bed, and as much out of routine as anything else, I
picked up the notebook that we were keeping as a fam-
ily. Instantly I recognized my father's handwriting. I fought
tears as I imagined my father writing in the quiet trying to
form the words as a message to all of us.

"(Personal note to my son from my heart). Jeff, I
haven't made any entries in this book, but I included
the prayer on the next page for the entire family to rely
on. When you are well enough, I will tell you about a lot
of tough times that Mom and I have gone through. The
many blessings that we've received are too numerous to
even try to count. I thank God every day for my beautiful

family. Just look at the blessings of my son-in-law, Chuck, and the beautiful daughters-in-laws that God brought to our family. Of course we must realize the goodness of our Lord for the grandchildren. Your sisters and brothers have been praying with sincerity and hope. Your brother-in-law and sisters-in-laws have really been concerned and are positive that you're going to return to us as the same Jeff. We must not forget all of your uncles and aunts and the many friends pulling for you. I know you'll make out okay. Jeff, this prayer got me through a lot of hard times.

Prayer to St. Jude

"Most holy apostle, St. Jude, faithful servant and friend of Jesus, the church honors and invokes you universally, as the patron of hopeless cases, of things almost despaired of. Pray for me, I am so helpless and alone. Make use I implore you, of that particular privilege given to you, to bring visible and speedy help where help is almost despaired of. Come to my assistance in this great need that I may receive the consolation and help of heaven in all my necessities, tribulations, and sufferings, particularly in Jeffrey's recovery, and that I may praise God with you and all the elect forever. I promise O blessed St. Jude, to be ever mindful of this great favor, to always honor you as my special and powerful patron, and to gratefully encourage devotion to you. Amen.

"To the Family: Pray for Jeff's recovery as your special intention. I've had this prayer for the last forty or so years. I've certainly had some bad situations, but God has given me so many blessings, and you are each one of them. Love, Dad.

During the course of the day, the discussion of Jeff's care began to center around talk of a rehabilitation center in Erie. The very meaning of the word "rehabilitation" buoyed our spirits. There was a long way to go, but with our love, he would be sustained. There was no doubt about it.

Despite the discussion of rehab, I couldn't shake the sleeplessness. In the late afternoon, I closed my eyes in the chair beside the hospital bed and remembered the dream that I'd had the night before. I had dreamed of Jeff, standing hard and strong, holding Rocco in one arm and Farrah in the other while Johnny attempted to jump on his back. Jeff had been smiling from ear to ear, and with the words of the prayer to St. Jude running through my mind, I thought back to another time and place. It was a day when I realized how happy my brother was with the life he'd been building. Perhaps the recall was spurred by my dream of seeing Jeff, once more, holding his children. In any regard, it simply tore at my insides as I remembered.

***

The ups and downs of life presented themselves in surprising fashion as Jeff and Lynn settled into their new life together. The initial euphoria of Lynn's first pregnancy turned to extreme hurt and disappointment when she lost the baby a month after conception.

"It's amazing," Jeff said as he called me with the news. "We went from the penthouse to the outhouse in about a span of three seconds. I feel so bad for Lynn."

"Yeah, me too," I said. "You can do like we did when we thought we wanted another kid."

"What's that?" Jeff asked.

"We went and got a dog."

"Did it help?" Jeff asked.

"It helped me," I said. "But Kathy wasn't really placated. Nine months later Sam was born."

"At least you got a dog out of the deal," Jeff joked.

Twenty minutes later there was a knock at the door. Jeff and Lynn stood together on the threshold, sharing a smile.

"What's going on?" I asked.

"We're going to the SPCA to pick out a dog," Jeff announced.

A couple of hours later, we were heading home with a beautiful Lab sharing the ride.

"What're you going to name him?" I asked.

"We have a name all picked out," Lynn said. "It's the perfect name. Happy."

A number of years later, I finally heard the secret behind the naming of the dog. On a Saturday afternoon in mid-December, Jeff called me for some help. He was working hard to prepare for Johnny's birthday party, and he wondered if I had a few spare moments to help him out.

"I'm trying to cook and these kids are driving me nuts. Lynn is working today, and I just can't get Rocco to settle down."

"Do you have beer?" I asked.

"What do you think? Hurry up."

I made the short trip and Jeff met me at the door with Rocco in one hand and a Heineken Light in the other. The beer was already uncapped.

"Take them both," he said.

I reached for Rocco, who immediately swung at me and called me "Poop."

"My God, this kid weighs a ton," I said after the shift was made.

"I know, and he always wants me to hold him. It kills my back."

We headed for the basement where Jeff had a full kitchen set up. Before we even hit the top steps I could smell the aroma of stuffed peppers. "What's on the menu today?" I asked.

Jeff smiled broadly. "Everything," he said. "You'll gorge

yourself for sure."

The downstairs play area was covered with toys. John and Farrah were on the floor in the other room, racing a large yellow car back and forth across the floor. The family dog, Happy, was curled up asleep in the center of it all. Rocco and I made our way to the middle of the commotion as Jeff removed a large pan of stuffed peppers from the oven.

"I made over a hundred peppers," Jeff said. "We have roast pork, a little pasta, a tomato salad and a platter of meats and cheeses. You better have a couple of beers now because you aren't going to be able to move after you eat."

I set Rocco on the floor next to beautiful Farrah, and after rubbing all of their heads and calling John a "donkey," I headed back to the kitchen. I watched Jeff chop an onion in record time and add it to the tomato salad.

Suddenly there was a yelp from the other room and I headed in to see Rocco pulling on Happy's tail. I broke up the one-sided fight and scooped Rocco up in my arms.

"Be nice to Happy," I said.

Rocco's wide smile was too much to deny, but a question popped into my head.

"Why'd you name that dog Happy?" I asked.

Jeff was straining the pasta. He drained the water, grabbed a quick sip of beer, and shrugged as if I were completely out of my mind. "We named him after the Bruce song," he said. "That and we wanted to capture the great spirit around here. Don't I look happy?"

I lifted my beer in a toast.

"You didn't have to cook a feast," I said. "A lot of people, especially when they have young kids, just get pizza and wings for a party."

Jeff laughed me off. "I'm a chef," he said. "I can't serve pizza and wings."

I returned Rocco to the floor and he immediately headed back to Happy, who had gained his feet and was running to get out of the way. John and Farrah joined in the fun and before too long all three were chasing the dog all around the basement. I was in close pursuit, but the entire parade struck me as funny.

"Happy, huh?" I laughed.

"We should've named it 'This Sucks,'" Jeff joked.

Three hours later, the plates were in the sink. Chuck and I were teammates in a beer-pong game against Jeff and Chris Heinold. The dog was curled up at Jeff's feet. The kids were running around the table, stopping the action every now and then to talk to Jeff. We resumed the game after one such break and Jeff's serve banged hard off the beer can positioned in the center of the table. He held onto the ball until Chuck and I could have a swig of beer. As I lifted the can, I recalled our conversation about the naming of the dog.

"Chow down that beer, wide load," Jeff called to me. "You're only cheating yourself."

I sipped the beer and caught his eye. He was smiling.

'Happy' was the perfect name for a dog in that loving family.

***

On March 1st, as I drove to the hospital again, I wondered who would be joining me at Jeff's bedside.

"If he can keep battling, I can keep battling," I said to the inside of my car.

The early morning air was frigid. I parked my car and took a deep breath, sucking the cold air into my lungs. "Keep me strong, today, God." I begged as I punched the elevator button. "And I'll take some good news if you have any."

Entering Jeff's room, I was greeted with the same still, silent figure in the bed. As had been the case for the better part of a couple of weeks, Jeff's eyes were open, but he made no response to my entrance.

"Morning, pal," I said.

I touched his right hand and gently rubbed the side of his face. Jeff closed his eyes as if to acknowledge I was there, but was that just a reaction to my hand on his face? His face was heavy with stubble. I wondered if they would bother to shave him anytime soon, or if that was our job.

Bitter frustration raced through my heart and mind. I wondered about the nurses and if they'd even checked on him in the last few hours. In a span of just a few seconds, I questioned every aspect of the care he was receiving. Was this how his life was supposed to go? Would there be a morning when I'd show up and find him sitting up in bed, waiting for someone to bring him his breakfast?

I continued to squeeze my brother's hand. I wanted to remain positive.

"God, can you hear me?" I whispered. "We have a big day today," I said to Jeff. "We're going to listen to a little Bruce. I brought Devils & Dust."

Jeff's eyes closed and opened. A small sign that he recognized what I'd said?

"I'm going to sing to you," I said. My voice cracked and again I realized that perhaps I was just too tired to pull it off. "No one loves you more than me, pal," I said. Tears threatened my eyes, but I knew that they would go unnoticed, and that was the real shame of it all.

Over the course of the next hour there were at least two nurses who'd stopped by to check Jeff and clear some of the built-up congestion. I was forced out into the hall during these examinations because I just couldn't handle the coughing that ravaged him. I was just so sick of coffee, so tired of listening to the never-changing prognosis.

"So I'm not getting any strength today, huh, God?" I whispered in the quiet hallway.

It was just a little before 8 a.m. when I decided to put the Bruce CD into the small boom box. I would work Jeff's arms and legs as best as I could. The staff had informed us that having him move was vitally important, and I thought of my sisters who had taken to the task as though they were working their own muscles.

The first sounds of the CD startled me to life, and I sang softly as I lifted Jeff's arms off the bed. I wondered if he could hear Bruce's voice, or my voice for that matter. I imagined that he would certainly cringe at the thought that I was singing to him, but like it or not, that was what he was getting.

For the next twenty minutes, I sang, cried and raised Jeff's arms. First I moved his left arm, then the right, then I sang the chorus, and I cried my way through it all. Did he know that I was crying? Was my voice driving him crazy? Did he recognize the sound of his favorite entertainer?

It didn't matter much anyway because the CD began to skip and then stopped altogether.

"Bruce is done," I whispered.

The silence in the room tore a hole straight through me. I continued to lift Jeff's arms. His eyes were wide open; too open. He showed no sign of recognition whatsoever.

"Dear God," I whispered.

They were just two simple words, but they prompted something inside my tired mind. I turned away from the bed and looked out the window. The morning sun was rising in the cloudy sky. It looked cold out there. Way too cold.

"How about the Our Father?" I said.

200

The words of the prayer came quickly, tumbling out of my mouth as they'd done nearly every day of my life. Did God hear me now?

I lifted Jeff's right hand and held it in my own as I said the words, crying my way through each one.

"Thy will be done," I said, and it hit me like a bolt of lightning through that hospital window. I remembered Jeff saying those words to me on at least a couple of occasions. "Oh God," I cried. "Thy will be done."

I hurried away from the bed and fell into the easy chair in the corner of the room. For the first time since he'd been brought to the hospital, I cried for all that I was worth.

Can you hear me now, God?

There was only so much crying I could do. After a month of unbelievable pain, I felt as though I could not reach another level of grief. Yet sitting in the chair, out of Jeff's line of vision, I cried for all that I was worth, and I wondered why no one was coming to save me.

As it turned out, my bedside relief was a long time in coming. John, Mom and Lynn were in route to Erie to check out the rehab facility. Dana and Lisa were watching the children, and Jim was still suffering from the effects of the gout. The first visitor that day turned out to be Jeff's best friend at work, Paul Rose.

Paul checked in on Jeff and then visited with me for a long while. He told me about the beautiful shawl that was on Jeff's bed, explaining that it had been a gift from a Gow School friend. The prayer shawl was handmade by Jacob and Martha Podyma.

"The students are besides themselves with worry," Paul said. "They absolutely adore your brother."

"That seems to be the consensus," I said.

As Paul sat beside me, I considered the day when Jeff had invited me to visit the Gow School.

Not long after he had settled in at Gow, he called to invite me to tour the campus. Of course, true to his nature, Jeff was thrilled to share his excitement. "Come on down and follow the long driveway to the back of the dining hall. You'll see my car parked out back next to the Dumpster," he said.

"How will I know which door to come in?" I asked.

"You'll know."

I made the fifteen-minute drive from my home, wondering about what sort of surprise he had ready for me. Telling me that I'd know where he was located sounded like one of his great pranks, and I was certainly laughing as I parked the car next to his because he waited for me to pull up by shooting baskets, all decked out in his chef's uniform, complete with a toque blanche.

"You get to shoot baskets?" I asked. "Boy, what a tough job you have."

Jeff tossed the ball to me and I took a shot from about fifteen feet away. I left it about a foot and a half short of the basket.

"Still a great player," he said.

We headed into the dining hall. He gave me a quick tour and handed me a wrapped sandwich for lunch.

"This is a great place," he said. "The kids are just awesome. I bust everyone's chops all day long. My boss is terrific, too. I'd introduce you to Brad and Paul but they won't be back for a while."

"That's all right. I'll come back again someday."

Jeff laughed. "Funny you should say that because I set up a book-signing for you here. They want you to come in and speak to the English class, and then they'll have you speak to everyone at the morning assembly."

"Yeah, maybe," I said.

"Maybe, my ass," he replied. "I already told them you'd do it."

On the morning of the book signing I was more than a little apprehensive. Through the years I had a lot of book signings that fell way short of my expectations, and I figured that I probably wouldn't sell a whole lot of books to a group of students. Yet about three steps into the door, I knew that things were going to be different on this visit.

"I love your brother," one kid said to me as I passed in the hall.

"You must laugh all day long with Jeff the Chef as your brother," another kid said.

I worked through a short presentation about writing and the publishing process in the English class and then threw it open to questions.

"Do you like the Yankees, too?"

"Does Jeff cook for you?"

"Are you the brother that bets football games with Jeff?"

"Do you guys really eat sauce every Sunday?"

I laughed my way through each of the questions. I had shown up at the school believing that the students might see me as a big-shot writer, but they were definitely more interested in me as the guy who had the privilege of being the brother to the greatest guy they ever met.

At the assembly, the headmaster, Brad Rogers, introduced me to the entire school and asked if I'd say a few words. Jeff had not yet joined the assembly, but just as I tested the microphone, he entered. A group of students in one area of the hall began to clap, and I couldn't help but smile. He was like a rock star to those kids!

Over the next half an hour, I spoke to the students about writing, living life to the fullest and doing their work to the best of their abilities. There was little doubt that the speech was going over well, but it became wildly successful when I relayed the story about nearly blowing my colon out after eating one of Jeff's meals.

"He's the best cook in the world," one of the kids shouted out. "But he likes the Yankees."

"You know," I said, "I've never seen Jeff so happy about going to work, but now I know why he loves the Gow School so much. He's found another 150 people to listen to his jokes and put up with his crap."

The kids all clapped for my brother and me. Looking out at Jeff from my place behind the podium, I saw a mixture of pride and true happiness in his eyes. He tipped his chef's cap to the cheering students, and as he looked back at me, I knew he saw the same emotions reflected in my eyes. I'd never been more proud of him than I was at that moment. He was a real superstar to those kids, and he loved them as much as they loved him.

Paul met me at the side of the podium. "I can't believe the love they have for him," I said.

"Sure you can," Paul answered. "Everyone who's ever met him loves him."

***

Paul stayed at the hospital with me through the early afternoon hours but left when Chris and Andrea Heinold and lifelong friend Tom Rybak joined me for a couple of hours. During their visit the nurses placed a sling around Jeff and lifted him out of the bed. They placed Jeff in a chair in an effort to get his muscles moving, but what should have been considered a step in the right direction brought more anxiety. Jeff couldn't hold his head up, his legs were pencil thin and to see him being lifted was almost too much to bear. I saw the pain in Chris' eyes, and while Tom tried hard to be encouraging, we were all stunned by the sight. Jeff's rehab was going to be a long, slow process, and we were not guaranteed anything in the end.

By the early evening I was on my way home. Jim and Chuck had joined Corinne at Jeff's bedside, and I was asked, very nicely, to go home and get some rest. John and Lynn had both checked in to inform us about the rehab center, and we were all excited with the possibility that Jeff would begin working hard to make it back to us.

The evening sky was charcoal gray, and it dawned on me that I had missed the entire day. I had left home in darkness and I was returning under even darker skies, if that were possible.

Kathy greeted me at the door with a long hug and a quick kiss. The boys each checked in on us, one after another, expressing their love in the usual manner.

"When you get down, remember that you're loved," Kathy said.

"You know love might not be enough," I said. "Tonight I feel like I might need a couple of dirty martinis to get me through."

"Go for it," Kathy said. "Maybe it'll help you sleep a little."

Three hours later, I was in the middle of mixing martini number three. Kathy and the kids were in bed, and I was alone with my memories, which brought a smile to my face and relief to my slightly foggy mind.

Many of the schemes in Jeff's life started with just a simple thought that he fostered, perfected and then presented to his simple mark. He always dreamed big, however, and usually was able to talk you into doing what he envisioned.

"Hey, get a plane ticket," he told me one spring morning in the late 1990s. He was calling from college in Norfolk, Virginia. "I set up a book signing for you at the school."

"Jeff, I'm not flying all the way to Virginia to sell three books to your friends," I said.

"Yes, you are," he responded. "I already set it up. You're speaking to the English class, they're having a reception and then we're going out drinking."

I was extremely hesitant. I was on the verge of getting

married, and life was as busy as could be. A trip to Norfolk wasn't in the cards.

"You only live once," Jeff said. "Imagine how much you'll hate yourself if you don't visit me at college."

"How many books can I possibly sell to pay for a plane ticket?" I asked.

"Sell one," he said. "Who cares? It gives you the chance to see me working down here."

So I made the trip. There was little chance that I wouldn't. The book signing was a modest event, and I read from the new book to a group of assembled students. The reading was certainly forgettable, but the food was not. As I spoke, a huge tray of stuffed hot peppers was passed in front of me. While in mid-speech, I took one from the tray. Stuffing it into my mouth in front of the group of students, I actually gasped.

"My God!" I said. "Who made these?"

Jeff's smile told me that his hand had been on those peppers. He was sitting there looking so proud that I nearly broke into tears.

"The greatest stuffed peppers ever," a girl in the front row said.

The rest of the visit was actually quite subdued. There was no doubt about it; Jeff was on a certain path.

I finished the third martini and called Corinne to check on Jeff one more time.

"We've been working hard," Corinne said. "We keep doing our exercises and we scratched a couple of lottery tickets together. We didn't win, but I think our luck is going to turn. Hang in there, Cliffy. We're still in it together."

"I know," I said. "But whoever said that alcohol could make you forget your problems was a real asshole. I'm on my third martini and it's just getting worse. I'm just replaying one memory after another."

"Then have four," Corinne said. "That'll make you stop

thinking."

Perhaps I should have listened to my sister, but I barely finished the third before falling into bed. I was planning on visiting the hospital in the morning, and I needed a bit of rest, but the ever-present memories stifled my plan to drift off to sleep. I tossed and turned and remembered. I thought of how hard Jeff and Lynn had worked to make their house a home.

In May of 2003, Jeff and Lynn were just a month away from adding another child to their lives. Jeff actually began his telephone conversation with those words after stirring my entire house awake at 6 a.m. on Saturday.

"What time are you going to be here?"

"What're you talking about?" I asked.

"My cousin Tony, my brother John, my brother Jim, my brother-in-law Chuck, and my friend Mike are all coming by to help me pour concrete. Is my other brother Cliff coming, too?"

Wiping sleep from my eyes and fully comprehending the question, I realized that he had phrased it in such a manner that I didn't have a lot of wiggle room to get out of helping.

"Of course, I'll understand if you can't make it," he said. "I have another kid on the way in about a month, and I really need your help, but if you have other things to do, I'll understand."

I laughed. "What time?"

"The first truck just pulled up," he said. "Bring your wheelbarrow and leave your whining at home. It's time to work! Remember, it's the quality of the moments that take your breath away!"

For the next few hours, I wheeled concrete as the rest of the crew worked to form the porch and set the sidewalk. We took just one short break all morning as we waited on the arrival of a second concrete truck.

During that break, Jeff, John, Jim and I talked about the arrival of our niece Paige, who'd been born to our sister Carrie just a month before.

"Paige weighed nine pounds and four ounces," Jeff said. "Can you imagine?"

Jeff's eyes flashed a true sense of wonder. He was considering the fact that his own family would be adding a member in a short time. He looked around his backyard and by looking in his eyes I could tell that he was thrilled with the direction of his life and the idea that our family was as close as ever. He set his bottle of water down and disappeared into the house. Moments later, with Lynn by his side, Jeff held his son John close to the newly poured concrete. Despite John's loud, shrieking protests Jeff pressed John's right hand into the mix. He scrawled the date into the space below the handprint.

"There! We'll be able to see that forever," he said.

I had turned away from the sight because I hadn't wanted Jeff to make fun of the tears in my eyes.

In my warm bed, I turned my pillow over, punched it, and tried hard to block out the next memory, but I didn't fight it hard enough, and it came back to me in full color.

***

The family get-together in early June of 2003 was significant to the Fazzolari's for a number of reasons. On a beautiful summer day we all gathered to share Dad's pasta and greet the new addition to the family as Carrie proudly showed off her lovely newborn daughter Paige.

Jeff and I were seated on the porch in the backyard, sipping water and gazing out to the baseball game being played on the same field where we had played game after countless game. My sons, Matt and Jake, were playing with Jim's boy, James, and John's daughters Nicole and Andrea. John was serving as the pitcher for both teams, and the sounds of joy were echoing across the yard to our ears.

"It's awesome, ain't it?" Jeff asked. He was lacing up his sneakers to join the game. "Our kids playing together on the same field we played on."

"Yeah, it's the circle of life," I said.

"Like the Lion King?" Jeff asked. "Are you quoting me the freaking Lion King? Come on, let's go play."

"What about your back?" I asked.

"My back will never stop me from playing with my kids."

I followed Jeff into the backyard. He immediately ran toward my son Jake, who picked up the ball and threw it at his uncle. For the next three hours, we played. Jeff's team won, of course, but the fun for the day was just beginning.

"How about a wheelbarrow race?" he asked as we headed back toward the house.

"What's a wheelbarrow race?" I asked.

As soon as the words left my mouth, I realized that I'd made a mistake.

"We have two wheelbarrows," he said. "John will push me in one and Jim can push you in the other one. We'll race to the woods and back."

"That's stupid," I said.

By now, my mother, father and our wives had all joined the discussion.

"I'll do it," Jim said. "Come on, all you have to do is get in. I'm doing the work."

"We're going to race a hundred yards in a wheelbarrow?" I asked. "Someone is going to end up crippled. I'm a thirty-eight-year-old man."

I was fighting a losing battle. My father had already returned to the scene with the second wheelbarrow.

"Climb in," Jim said.

By the time Jeff and I had settled into the wheelbarrows, the entire family had gathered. Our children were cheering us on. Mom and Dad were placing bets and taking photos. Our wives were counting down the seconds until the start of the race.

"Just don't dump me," I said to Jim.

I tried to settle into the bottom of the rusty blue wheelbarrow. Jeff's eyes were filled with the same sort of excitement that I'd seen from him on the morning that he was making Kool-Aid in the center of our parent's kitchen when he'd been just two-years-old.

"You're about to lose again," he said. We bumped fists just as our wives' count reached zero.

The race was pretty much over in the first twenty yards. John, buoyed by his chanting partner, raced the one hundred yards in about eight seconds. Jim pumped hard, the veins on his neck standing out as he tried to move the wheelbarrow with me in it. He dumped it after about ten steps, tumbling over the top of the handle and onto my back as we thundered to the ground. I'm not sure that I've ever seen my mother and father laugh quite so hard.

Walking toward the house, I was busy examining the cuts on my right arm. Jeff ran up behind me and slapped me hard on the butt as he raced ahead.

"You lost again!" he cried. "We get so sick of whipping your ass!"

The great wheelbarrow race concluded a nearly perfect day.

***

I don't remember falling asleep that night, but I was awake just a few minutes after 4 a.m. I sat on the edge of the bed with a pounding head and a heart that seemed to be beating a little too hard. I thought of the wheelbarrow race and laughed.

I headed to the refrigerator for a bottle of cold water, and as I chugged the water, I thought only of Jeff and my love for him. "He's going to be all right," I whispered to the dark. "We're counting on a miracle."

Chapter XIII – Counting on a Miracle

March 2-March 3, 2009   Faith is daring the soul to go beyond what the eyes can see.   William Newton Clark

On Sunday morning March 2, I made the drive to the hospital for the thirty-second straight day. Despite the fact that I was doing what I'd taught myself to do over the course of the month, I knew that it was time for a drastic change. Martini remnants were clouding my vision a bit, but my prayer with Jeff on the morning before, 'Thy Will Be Done,' had propelled me to a new way of thinking.

Nearly eight years before, as my son Jake struggled with a life-threatening tumor, a friend of mine had explained that negative thoughts were supplied courtesy of Satan and that I needed to seriously reshape my thinking to accentuate the positive and rely on God. From where I was sitting behind the wheel of that car heading to the hospital again, the problem was that God hadn't given us much in the past days. Jeff, while initially showing improvement, was still really suffering. An airplane had crashed, killing fifty in western New York and the economy was in the tank, as we were all reminded on a daily basis. How in the hell was I going to find the positive?

The first of my changes was to involve Springsteen as a way of pepping up the morning drive. I put the Working On A Dream CD into the player and allowed the sounds to cover me as I drove. I knew that listening to Springsteen was just step one, but I definitely had a plan.

I headed straight to the bedside and was immediately buoyed by the fact that Jeff was wide awake. He closed his eyes and furrowed his brow as though he were saying good morning in a horribly tragic manner.

"Good morning, pal," I said. "Nurse Cliffy on duty. It's 6 o'clock on Sunday morning and I'm thinking about pasta already."

Jeff's eyes were centered on my face, but I wondered if he was truly seeing me or if he could comprehend. I took the red washcloth off his forehead and saw that he was sweating profusely. I wondered if a nurse had checked in on him recently. The cloth was warm, although the room was ice cold.

How in the hell was I supposed to stay positive?

I headed to the bathroom, ran cold water over a clean washcloth and headed back to the bed. When I set the cloth on Jeff's head, he seemed to relax a bit, and he closed his eyes. My mind immediately shifted to prayer. Thankfully, we had both calmed a bit.

I sat in the chair beside the bed and considered all that would happen in the next couple of days. Lynn, Mom and John had returned with mostly favorable reviews of the rehab facility in Erie, but there was so much work to be done. Would Jeff be accepted early in the week, as we all believed? Was he stable enough to make the trip? How would we handle not seeing him each and every day as he was nursed back to health, for a stretch as long as a year? He was supposed to be coming home, not going further away to a place that was a ninety-minute drive from our home!

I felt the negative creeping in and threatening to overwhelm me. Jeff's left leg was showing, and it was so thin that I got out of the chair and covered it. He needed to start the rehab. We couldn't just let him lie in that bed and waste away. If this was what needed to be done, we would do it.

Jeff's nurse for the day finally checked in at just around 8 a.m. Of course, this nurse was the guy who rubbed me the wrong way, and despite my search to find the posi-

tive, the man's early morning performance was madden-
ing.

"He's sweating profusely," I said, "and he seems to be
in some pain. I'm not sure what it is, but he sort of cringes
with pain, almost as if he has bad gas."

"Huh," the nurse said.

I waited for him to finish his thought, but there wasn't
anything more to come.

"Huh?" I asked. "Is that what you're thinking?"

"I'll let his doctors know," he said. "His temp is a little
high, but it's not alarming."

"Well, the sweat on his forehead is alarming to me," I
said.

"I got you," the nurse said. He headed out of the room
without glancing in my direction again.

"Huh!" I said.

Jim called me to update me on his bitter battle with
the gout. The medicine was making him extremely ill and
the lack of any sleep at all was catching up with him. I
begged him to stay where he was and get a bit of rest.

"We're going to need you to make a few trips to Erie,"
I said. "And for God's sake, we have enough to worry
about. You have to get healthy."

Jim's call was immediately followed by consecutive
calls from John, Chuck, Carrie and Mom. I updated each,
trying very hard to keep a positive tone to my voice. We
spoke of the coming week, and I asked Chuck to tell the
ever-diligent Corinne to schedule our days so that Jeff
was not alone during the first week of his rehab. Chuck
assured me that Corinne would get it done, and I had no
doubt.

Thankfully, around 10 a.m. the doctor on duty stopped
by. I had noticed the man before, but his name escaped
me. "I hear Jeff is a little warm this morning," he said.

"Yeah, it must be a real emergency," I said. "It only took

you guys a couple of hours to get here."

The doctor ignored my sarcasm. He looked at Jeff for a few moments and explained that he would be clearing the trach.

"I'm going to head to the cafeteria," I said. "I can't handle watching that." The doctor smiled as though I were being absolutely ridiculous. "Is he doing okay?" I asked.

"He needs rehab," he said. "He needs to get those muscles working again. His elevated temperature is to be expected with his injury."

We both glanced at Jeff's form in the bed. His face was still unshaven, the sweat was beading up again on his face and a cough shook his entire body.

"He's a good athlete," I said, "and a real strong guy."

"That's why he's progressed so far," the doctor said.

I wasn't quite sure how much Jeff had progressed, but on the way to the cafeteria, I considered Jeff as an athlete. We had played so many games together through the years, and he had won most of them.

I remembered when Jeff returned from his schooling in Norfolk for a quick break. As usual we called a bunch of good friends together. Jeff Renaldo, Pete Renaldo, Jim, Joe, Jeff and Jan Mathis, Jan Warren, Jeff Popple and Tony Puntillo were all part of the group that got together to play ball on the day before Thanksgiving in Collins.

For three hours we had competed hard on the basketball court. Jeff's recreation team was pitted against mine, and we guarded one another all day long. He had scored more points during the course of the day, and his team had ended up winning on a last-second shot from the corner. Jeff had released the shot over the top of my extended hand.

As we dressed for the trip to my parent's home for a dinner of pasta and meatballs, Jeff let me have it. Over and over he relived the final play, doing an imitation of an announcer's voice and the roar of a crowd.

"Jeff Fazzolari gets the ball in the corner. He dribbles once. He dribbles twice. He looks deep into the eyes of the slow-moving creature guarding him, and he brings the ball up over his head. The mammoth creature lunges at him as Jeff releases the shot. WHAP! The sound of the net echoes through the arena as the crowd goes absolutely bat-shit."

I had learned many years before not to react to my brother when he was in the middle of teasing me. I pretended that he didn't even exist.

"Ah, come on, don't be like that," Jeff said. "Someone has to lose, right? Can you follow me to the gas station? I'm burning oil and I don't think I'll make it to Mom and Dad's."

Without saying a single word, I headed to the lot. From the locker room to the parking lot, Jeff did a variation on his broadcast of the winning shot. The end of each sentence was punctuated with the word WHAP!

I followed Jeff's car into the gas station parking lot. He opened the hood, poured a quart of oil into the engine, all the while doing a recap of the game-winner.

"I've had enough," I said finally. "Let's just get to Mom and Dad's."

The gas station was located about five miles away from the house on an open road that allowed for over-the-speed-limit travel.

"Say, I have an idea," Jeff said as he leaned into my car window on the passenger's side. "We'll race home."

"I'm not racing you home," I said.

"We'll do it this way," he said. "If you beat me, I won't mention the game-winning shot ever again. You in?"

"No, I'm not racing."

Jeff walked around to his driver's side door. "It's settled

then. Last one home is a rotten egg."

He jumped in behind the wheel and stood on the pedal as his car screeched from the lot. Out of the corner of my eye, I noticed that the hood on his car had not been fully latched. In an instant, I imagined him flying down Shirley Road oblivious to anything but beating me home. I could almost see the hood flipping up, obscuring his vision and causing him to go careening off the road. I did the only thing I could; I stepped down hard on the accelerator, blew the horn and flashed my lights in an effort to get him to pull over and slam the hood. Jeff didn't get the message. Instead, he stomped down harder on the pedal and his taillights grew smaller.

"Stupid bastard!" I screamed to the inside of my car. I slowed a bit, but was still going nearly 75 mph on the posted 55 mph road when the flashing lights of the police car drew my attention to the rearview mirror.

The police officer all but ran up to the side of my car.

"Do you understand that you're twenty miles an hour over the speed limit?"

"I'm sorry, sir," I said. "My brother was in front of me and his hood wasn't latched properly. I was trying to catch him to get him to pull over and shut the hood."

"There wasn't a car in front of you," the cop said.

"He was going about a hundred," I said.

The cop removed his sunglasses and very calmly mentioned that he didn't believe me.

Fifteen minutes later, I entered my parent's home, carrying a yellow piece of paper that would cost me a night in court and at least $100. Jeff was seated at the kitchen table regaling everyone with his game-winning shot.

"What took you so long, pumpkin?" he asked.

I held the speeding ticket up high, and he nearly fell off his chair in a fit of laughter. "WHAP!" he squealed.

I laughed as hard as he did although it cost me over a

hundred dollars to try and chase him home.

***

On Sunday evening I sat on the couch with my children all around me. We were watching episodes of The Simpsons and sharing the laughs. Sam was sitting real close, going through each line of dialogue with me. I closed my eyes for a long moment and allowed the positive vibes to consume me. I considered the fact that I was laughing with my boys as I continued to weep inside my heart. It was the strangest of all feelings, but Sam, Jake and Matt's love surrounded me. Their love propelled me forward in what promised to be a week of monumental change as Jeff began his rehab work.

As I prepared for bed, I decided to check my e-mail one more time. Carrie had checked in with a message that sent me to bed in a dizzying fit of prayer.

"Hi, Cliffy. I just found an e-mail that I sent to Jeff back in November. It's a beautiful novena prayer that I really meant for his eyes only as he struggled through his back pain and the loss of his friend Matt. I'm thinking you can use the positive energy right now. Anyway, here's the message sent and received! Talk to you tomorrow, Love Carrie."

I read the e-mail, thinking back in time to how Jeff had been feeling and how much Carrie loved him. The idea of praying as hard as I could possibly pray entered my mind as I read and re-read the e-mail.

"Jeff, for some reason, felt like you might need this. You're the only one I'm sending it to. Love you, Carrot.

"You were chosen to receive this novena. The moment you receive it say: Our Father who art in heaven, hallowed be Thy name, Thy kingdom come, Thy will be done, on earth as it is in heaven, give us this day our daily bread and forgive us our trespasses as we forgive those who trespass against us and lead us not into temptation but deliver us from evil. Amen.

"GOD WANTED ME TO TELL YOU it shall be well with you this coming year. No matter how much your enemies try this year, they will not succeed. You have been destined to make it and you shall surely achieve all your goals this year.

"For the remainder of 2008 and all of 2009, all your agonies will be diverted and victory and prosperity will be incoming in abundance. Today God has confirmed the end of your sufferings, sorrows and pain because He that sits on the throne has remembered you. He has taken away the hardships and given you JOY. He will never let you down.

"I knocked at heaven's door this morning. God asked me, 'My child! What can I do for you?' And I said, 'Father please protect and bless the person reading this message.'

"This is a Novena from Mother Theresa that started in 1952. It has never been broken. God does not know if you don't have any people to send it to. It's the effort and intent that counts.

I was saying the rosary as I drifted off to sleep. In between each of the Hail Marys I begged God to please listen to us. I didn't worry about not finishing the entire prayer as sleep descended on me. The angels would finish it for me.

***

During the course of the day on Monday the plans for Jeff's move from Mercy Hospital to the rehab facility in Erie were finalized. As a family, we debated the reasoning of such a move, but Lynn was doing her homework, making decisions that a wife and mother should never have to make. We were buoyed by the cooperation of the staff and the recommendations of the doctors. This was the move to make. Despite the fact that Jeff's progress could not be monitored from five minutes down the road, the longer road to him would not separate us. We would always be there for him, no matter what.

The telephone lines were really burning during the course of the day. John and Jim were to accompany Lynn to Erie to check Jeff into the facility. I was to be on hand at Mercy with Lynn to ensure that Jeff's transport was all set. There was a possibility that the trip could affect Jeff's stability, but safeguard measures would be in place.

I arrived at the hospital in the early morning hours, believing that Jeff would be on his way by ten a.m. I was also well aware that before the day was over, Jeff and I would be separated by hundreds of miles, as I was slated to work in Utica, New York, on Tuesday morning.

I made my way to Jeff's bed. His eyes were wide open and the ever-present sweat was covering his brow.

"Morning sunshine," I said. "Today is moving day. We're going to get you working a little."

Jeff's forehead furrowed and his now-frail body contorted as though he were experiencing tremendous stomach pains. The pain on his face was quickly transferred to my own heart.

"I know it sucks, buddy, but you really are getting there. Just a little more time. Just a little more rest."

His pain seemed to subside. A tear rolled down his left cheek. Earlier in the week there had been a discussion about whether or not Jeff was aware enough to understand our mental anguish. Was he crying because he was sad?

It was way too much to consider. I tried to chase the negative.

I glanced at the notebook that was left on the windowsill. Corinne had summed up the move by making one last entry: On to your next journey, pal. We will start a new book for your next phase of life. I love you, Love,

220

Corinne. PS – I will miss not seeing you every day, and holding your hand too.

By nine a.m. Lynn joined me in the room. I hugged her hello and we shared a troubled glance.

"We're doing the right thing here," she said.

"I believe so," I said. "We're flying blind, but he has to get moving. He's just lying there. He needs stimulation, right?"

Lynn nodded slowly. "It's what everyone is telling us."

Lynn edged closer to the bed. She touched the side of Jeff's face and kissed him over and over, soft kisses that caused Jeff's eyes to close; the pain that had been on his face slipped away. I was on the opposite side of the bed, fighting hard not to blubber at the sight.

"I'll get us a coffee," I whispered, wanting to give Lynn some time alone with Jeff.

I returned to the room about ten minutes later to find Lynn in conversation with a member of the neurological team.

"He's going to do well," the young woman said. "This type of injury takes a long time to battle through, but I really believe that Jeff is a good candidate for rehab."

The encouraging words were desperately needed, and I smiled at Lynn. "The only things that are bothering me," I said, "are the sweating and the pain that he seems to be in. He cringes and cries. It's breaking my heart."

"It's such a complicated matter," the woman said. "The temperature fluctuations are common in this type of injury, and he may be crying because he feels emotional. He's becoming more aware. The realization of what's happened is not easily handled. Yet he'll get there. I know he will."

When the woman excused herself, Lynn and I took our place at either side of the bed. Lynn's soft touch relaxed Jeff, and I spoke to my brother in whispered tones. "Buddy, we're all here. We'll always be here for you and you know that. You have a beautiful family, and we all love you. You have beautiful kids and a good wife. You have everything you need to get through this, and I promise you, you'll do it. You'll do it."

Lynn met with the transport team and the doctors, handling the necessary paperwork for the transfer. Jeff was not moved out of the room as scheduled at ten because Lynn wanted to be assured that his temperature was under control, and that Jeff was indeed stable enough for the long ride down I-90. Over and over again we were assured that all was well, and that Jeff was indeed in good hands.

Just before noon, Lynn and I stood in the back lot of Mercy Hospital as Jeff was loaded into an ambulance. I paused outside the door, glancing at the bed that held my brother's form. "I'll see you down there, buddy," I said. "Who loves you more than me?"

The driver closed the door, and Lynn and I shared a hug.

"We'll call you when he's settled," Lynn said.

John, Jim, Mom and Lynn followed the ambulance down I-90, and I headed off in the other direction for my work obligation in Utica, some four hours away.

I didn't do anything but cry through the first hour of my trip to Utica, but as the miles passed, I once more set to work on my own mind. It was a wonderfully clear day and the bright sunshine was causing havoc with my ability to see the road. I kept moving the visor in an effort to block the sun, but after a little while, I just let the sun bear down on me. There was no doubt that the rehab would be a monumental task that would place a heavy strain on all involved, but our family unit was just too strong to cave to that sort of pressure.

"We can do this!" I said.

The further I drove, the more the sadness and con-
fusion began to dissipate. The bright sun continued to
shine, and my telephone was my connection to the hearts
of my wife, my parents and each of my siblings. Before
too long, the only thing that I was feeling was determina-
tion. I dialed Carrie's number and spoke for a long time to
my baby sister. We spoke of love and togetherness and
hope. More than anything else, we discussed hope.

"You know, I keep thinking about one day in particular,"
Carrie said. "I keep thinking of a day nearly ten years ago
when Jeff and Lynn came to visit me after I was first mar-
ried. It was about this time of year, too. We all went out
the night before, shooting darts, playing the jukebox and
laughing. At one point, we even played air guitar together
in the middle of the bar in front of about a dozen other
patrons, laughing and shaking our heads, jumping up and
down, falling to our knees. It all ended in applause and
another round of drinks for us.

"Needless to say the next morning was rough. It was
especially rough when, at seven a.m. I heard the words,
'The heart is a bloom...' followed by the entire song
played over and over. It was right after U2 had released
Beautiful Day."

"Jeff loves that song," I said.

"Yeah, no kidding," Carrie said. "After the first six times,
I rolled over, and with a pounding headache, managed
to walk into the room where Jeff and Lynn were staying.
Jeff was seated at the computer, and when I walked in he
looked up and smiled.

"Good morning, sunshine!" he said, then started the
song again.

"What's wrong with you?" I asked.

"Jeff laughed. Wow, how hard he laughed."

"He's a beauty," I said. I could appreciate Carrie's recall
of the day because for the past month I'd been running

memories through my head day after long day.

"When I think about it I can clearly here the song, and I can still see his smile," Carrie continued. "I recall how he stood up, shirtless, with the crucifix hanging around his neck, a pair of shorts hanging loosely around his butt, and those long arms and legs, his face full of razor stubble, his eyebrows full and bushy, a chew in his lower lip. I see him raising those eyebrows, waiting for the moment in the song and then belting out the words, 'It's a beautiful day!'

"He played the song at least ten more times, until I was laughing and singing along, despite my headache. That's what I'm thinking about today. How he always pulled me in and made me enjoy every moment."

By the time Carrie finished her story, we were both crying.

"He told me to enjoy life instead of trying to understand it," I said.

"And that's how he lives," Carrie said.

"He's going to be fine," I said. "He's always managed to battle through it."

"I know," Carrie said.

As we said our good-byes, I decided once and for all to take Jeff's advice. He would get through his physical rehab, and I would adopt his mental philosophy. I was going to really start to enjoy life. I considered Jeff and Carrie and their special relationship, and it occurred to me that Jeff had that type of relationship with all of us. I thought of Carrie's wedding and how proud he'd been on that day.

***

Carrie was married on September 23rd, 2000. If there was a single day that brought forth all the love that Jeff had in his heart, it was his younger sister's wedding day. He worked hard with Corinne to set up a slide show presentation that would show Carrie's growth through the years. Of course, there was plenty of humor sprinkled in, and Jeff treasured the chance to say a few words to introduce the presentation.

Jeff spoke of how each sibling influenced Carrie through the years, breaking it down in hilarious fashion.

"Corinne taught Carrie how to smoke and break curfew and live life to the fullest. John taught Carrie strength and the ability to work through problems. Cliff taught Carrie that reading and writing is really a good thing. Jim taught Carrie the greatest lesson of all: that maybe the family needs a lawyer, and I, Jeff, taught Carrie that a brother and sister really can be best friends."

The gathering was still laughing at Jeff's joke about his brother Jim when he hit them with the line about his own relationship with Carrie. Jeff choked up as the words left his mouth, and the two hundred guests choked up right along with him. The slide show was presented and when it concluded, there wasn't a dry eye in the crowd.

The rest of the wedding reception could best be described as "The Jeff Show." He led a conga line of forty people through the entire hall, leading the line on top of tables and chairs and in front of Grandma Schryver, and he made sure that everyone in the line kissed the matriarch of the family.

He initiated the Thunder Road chair lift and screamed the last line to his crying sister. "So Carrie climb in, it's a town full of losers and we're pulling out of here to win."

As the evening came to a conclusion I walked outside the wedding hall with Jeff at my side.

"We're all married now," he said.

"Yeah, that was a good time," I said.

"We're doing good, huh?"

"We're doing real good," I said.

As the recollection of Carrie's wedding faded, I made the same life decision that I'd been trying to make for so long. "It starts now," I announced to the inside of my truck.

I grabbed the copy of Springsteen's Working on a Dream CD. I turned the volume up as loud as it could go, and the wailing sounds of Springsteen's guitar shook the speakers as the opening of Lucky Day blared.

"You told me to enjoy life, brother. I'm going to try. I really am."

Chapter XIV-The Last Carnival

March 04, 2009 - My God, My God, Why have you forsaken me? Matthew 27:46

On the morning of March 4, 2008, I prepared for my training as I thought about Jeff settling into his new digs. I didn't know how much they would work him on that first day, but he was in the place where they'd nurse him back to health.

There were at least fifty people sitting in the auditorium where I was to give a lesson on fall protection safety in construction. I took a deep breath and headed to the podium at the front of the room.

"'Morning everyone," I said.

The cell phone vibrated in my pocket, and I stepped back as I glanced at the name on the faceplate: Lynn.

"I'll be right back," I said to the class.

I stepped out of the room and made my way down a short hallway, ducking into a utility closet just off the auditorium. "What's up?" I asked.

"He's in decline," Lynn said through a sob.

"What do you mean?" I asked.

"John and Jim are meeting me, we're heading down there," Lynn said. "His heart rate was way too high this morning."

The tremor in Lynn's voice scared the holy hell out of me.

"He's all right, right?" I asked.

"They said 'decline,'" Lynn said.

Lynn's crying forced my legs to go weak. I placed my hand against the wall. How could I get there fast enough to make a difference? They were all working on him, right? It wasn't life threatening, was it?

I thought about the gathering of people waiting for me to get started. I stumbled out of the closet and down the hall. I poked my head into the room and summoned the owner of the company. I'm not even sure what I said, but his instruction was clear enough.

"Get out of here!" he said. "Do what you have to do!"

Before I even made it back into the hallway, the phone vibrated once more.

"Cliff, it's Mom. What's going on?"

"I don't know. I think he has a high heart rate. He'll be okay."

Mom couldn't respond. I didn't want to use the word decline. It wasn't that bad, right?

"John and Jim are heading there with Lynn. I'm sure they're going to stabilize him." I said. "Just hang tight."

"Okay," Mom said, and we hung up.

I was doing my best to shield Mom, but the heartbreak was evident in her voice.

"Jesus, God! Are you kidding me?" I stepped back into the small closet. There were mops, brooms and empty buckets lying around. I kicked at the mop bucket, turning it on its side. "Are you fucking kidding me?" The words were no sooner out of my mouth when the phone vibrated again and I saw Jim's name come up.

"Are you sitting down?" he cried.

In that single moment, I knew that life had forever changed. The pain crippled me, and I slid down the wall to a kneeling position. I didn't want Jim to say the words, but he did. He did.

"Jesus, Cliff, Jeff died. He died!"

Every ounce of air was sucked from my lungs. I sat on the floor of a utility closet in Utica, New York, crying in disbelief, knowing that it was a pain that was being felt all over my world.

Jeff had spent a restless night at the rehab facility, but the high heart rate that was a concern in Buffalo became a major problem in Erie. The details didn't matter. I simply heard Jim's voice over and over in my mind, saying the words that hardly seemed fathomable.

Kathy called next. "Please, just drive safe," she cried. "Can you do it?"

"I don't know," I said. "I'm under control, though."

"Don't drive fast! Please be careful."

I wasn't worried about speed causing an accident. There wasn't anything I would accomplish by racing home. The problem I was having was that I wasn't sure I'd be able to hold my head up high enough to see over the steering wheel.

As I staggered to the parking lot, the morning sun was high in a clear blue sky. The air was crisp, and around me life was a bustle of activity. I couldn't see anyone or anything, however. All that mattered was my family, and the pain that we would now carry until the end of time.

I settled into the car, turned the radio off and slammed the steering wheel with my open hand. "This is never going to stop hurting!" I cried, and that statement sat trapped in the SUV as I traveled down the highway.

As I drove west toward my family, one other thought continued to cross my mind. "Why, God, why?"

The question just kept hammering away at my brain as I drove. Mile after mile I shouted to the interior of my car, "Why?"

It's funny, but there are times in life when we actually wish time away. I thought of all the times when I wished I were somewhere else, doing anything else. As I drove, the minutes were moving like months, the gnawing, crippling pain offering little more than the one word question: Why?

As I neared Buffalo, the pain of the loss changed from

a numbing wave of incoherent thought to a more com-
prehensive hurt that overtook all of my senses. I spoke to
Jeff as though he were right beside me in that car, crying
so hard that I thought about pulling to the side of the road
to let it all out. I said each word of the collected thoughts
out loud, knowing that I would feel the pain of loss for the
rest of my days.

"You're supposed to be standing beside me as I roll
a three-foot putt by the hole, saying, 'Ah, that's a damn
shame.' You're supposed to call me on the phone after
winning a bet from me, telling me, 'You're so stuuuuuuuu-
pid.' You're supposed to call me after I step off of live tele-
vision and say, 'I know the camera adds ten pounds, but
how the hell many cameras did they have on you?' You're
supposed to be here. We are two trapeze artists, and I
stand with my wrist waiting for your hand. You're sup-
posed to be here for fifty more years, making fun of me,
rooting the Yankees on, by my side as Bruce sings for
us. You're supposed to be teaching me new recipes, and
we're supposed to compare notes on the wife and kids.
You're supposed to be calling me every day and getting
me involved in your scams. You're supposed to be invit-
ing me to pick NCAA teams out of a hat. You're supposed
to tell me, like you told me two days before you got sick,
that I should enjoy life instead of trying to understand it.
You're supposed to be hoisting your kids high and teach-
ing them all the best swear words. You're supposed to be
here, so proud of me and our other brothers and sisters.
You're supposed to call each of us on weekend mornings
just to catch up. You're supposed to cook me unbeliev-
able meals and laugh at how much I'm eating. You're
supposed to think right along with me on every pos-
sible subject imaginable. You're supposed to be my best
friend. You're supposed to be here, and hopefully in time,
I'll understand why you aren't. My dear brother, you left

me with one comfort and that's in knowing that I'll always know how you feel about something, and that's because our hearts always beat to the same rhythm. You're supposed to be here helping me to move this mountain of grief. You're supposed to be. And somehow, some way, some day, I know you will be. Because, I could always count on you."

The first embrace was too much to take. Mom was weeping so hard that I was sure that something had broken inside of her.

"It's going to be all right," I whispered.

Mom pushed back away from me. She looked at me as if I were an alien.

"No, it isn't," she cried. "It'll never be all right again."

"Love is our only chance, Mom," I said.

During the course of the next three days we spent every possible moment together as Jeff's friends gathered, and the home where we had all grown up was filled with visitors who offered condolences, food and as much love as we could handle, but as a family we were numbed, and virtually lifeless. This was Jeff who was gone! His death was fresh upon us, and we didn't have any idea how to react.

On the night before Jeff's funeral, the family spent six hours at the funeral parlor, literally shaking a thousand hands. Yet the wake left little comfort. The only words that truly comforted me came courtesy of the man who'd spent a number of nights guarding Jeff on the basketball court.

"Every time I think of him I smile," Jeff's buddy Jan Warren said.

I decided that I would try to make Jan's thought a daily mantra. I would smile for Jeff at least once a day for the rest of my life. Yet it seemed way too soon to start smiling now.

Returning to my parent's home, I felt a little like a walking zombie. By the expressionless faces of those gathered around me, I knew that I was not alone. The shock had not worn off, and it certainly didn't feel as if it ever would.

The rain was tumbling down hard and cold, and the chill of the evening air was wreaking havoc with my ability to think clearly. I had carried seven bags of garbage out of my parent's home, and my father was waiting in the garage with two more bags. I had made the trip from the curb to the house at least twice, and I was absolutely soaked to the bone. Yet I hadn't bothered to grab a jacket, and despite the cold rain, I was in no hurry to get the bags from my father's hands. I walked as slowly as I may have ever walked, letting the rain soak me, chill me and sting the back of my neck. It was almost as though I didn't want to get to the garage, where I'd see that sad expression in my father's eyes. The rain continued to hammer me. Dad was moving around, performing tasks, just doing his best to stay upright.

I took the two remaining bags from my father's hands. I couldn't avoid his eyes, and I saw so much hurt that I gasped for air. I was tired of breaking down. That was why I had allowed the rain to soak me. I needed to be cold. I wanted to be beaten down by the rain. My father handed the bags to me and said thank you.

"My sons have always helped me," he said. "Jeff was always ready to help me, but he won't be here anymore."

"I can get it, Dad," I said lamely, but his tearful eyes drew me to him. I dropped the bags and we hugged.

"It's never going to be the same again," he said.

The pain was absolutely unbearable for all, but shock, sleep depravation, plate after plate of food delivered by a wonderful town filled with family and friends and beer after beer pushed us through the ceremony associated with sending Jeff into a better world. The one word question, why?, kept hammering away in the minds of hundreds and hundreds of people who loved Jeff. He had arrived safe and sound at the rehab facility, but the rapid heart rate was too much to handle. Should we have left him in Buffalo? Was there anything we could have done? Had his care been mishandled in some way? How did a strong, healthy man suffer such an injury in the first place? Where was God? I wasn't alone in my attempt to find an answer, but there just weren't any answers forthcoming. Why?

There was little in life that prepared the family for the unbelievable pain that came with our loss. Tears fell in bucketfuls, and the sharp bite of anger was just around the corner. Bottles were drained in an effort to dull the pain, but the answer was right there in front of us all the time.

"Only love can teach us joy again," Carrie said.

It was a simple enough statement but one that carried so much truth that we began to search for love again, in one another's eyes.

On the night before Jeff's funeral, I lay in my bed, alternating between crying in pain and praying for strength. I tried so hard to make some sense, even a little bit of sense, out of it. In the backdrop of Carrie's simple sentence, I thought of love. My mind centered on the love that the family would need to make it through even a single week, but before long, I began to think of the love that Jeff had brought to our lives, and there was no greater love than the love Jeff held for his family. As a child, he provided an undying love and loyalty to his brothers, sisters and parents. There wasn't a single time when Jeff turned his back on his blood. As he grew to an adult, his love grew along with him. Jeff was always the force that generated larger gatherings of relatives, often making sure that his cousins living in other areas were not forgotten. Jeff was always on the telephone, speaking with the Switala family in Maryland, his favorite Uncle Jim, or the Fazzolari family in Gasport. He welcomed his brothers and sisters-in laws with open arms, and no one was exempt from his teasing or his love. He loved Corinne's husband Chuck as a brother, my wife Kathy, Jim's wife Lisa and John's wife Dana as sisters, and his love was certainly contagious. We all got caught up in the whirlwind of Jeff's love, and during the time of his memorial we needed desperately to remember his lesson to us: No distance is too far when it comes to sharing with those who we love.

When Jeff was married, his sense of family grew even sharper. He spoke so proudly and lovingly of the life that he and Lynn had made. His eyes would sparkle when he talked of Johnny, Farrah or Rocco. We were sure that his love was endless, and lying in that cold bed, with tears streaming down my face, I knew that it was. Jeff's love would be endless. We would not be separated. Not even by death. We are a family. I finally succumbed to sleep, dreaming of his love.

Chapter XV-The Rising

*There are some things that carry us through our lives;
there are people we can lean on and people we can love,
who lean on us, who love us too. Sometimes the people
who bring us that joy, who bring us that laughter, are-the
ones we lose to God. But with God comes Grace and in
our life we live with that Grace. We get through every day
for the sake of the one we so deeply miss. And we find
that pain can move us and that memories can comfort us
in ways that we never imagined.   Carrie Fazzolari*

On the morning of Jeff's funeral I woke with my mind
centered on one thing: I needed to stuff the hot peppers.
For many years Jeff had prepared stuffed hot peppers for
every occasion. True to his nature, he took the compli-
ments in stride, but all questions about the ingredients
were turned aside with a wave of the hand. In the end,
however, Jeff could not deny the recipe any longer, and
it was finally secured, via e-mail, after Carrie badgered
Jeff. I was not privy to the exchange of e-mails, but I was
included in the information sharing and on the morning
of Jeff's funeral, I prepared the peppers as he taught
me. Working quickly I cored each pepper, removing the
seeds, and washing them. In Jeff's note to Carrie, he had
included a playful dig about how I probably wouldn't wash
the peppers because I never bothered to wash myself.
The recollection brought a tear to my eyes, but I contin-
ued to work through it. I thought of Jeff's hands on every
pepper at every single gathering over the last ten years.
In a mixing bowl I added cream cheese, pork sausage,
Parmesan cheese, granulated garlic, fresh basil, black
pepper, parsley, onion, cayenne pepper, and finely diced
onion. I added a few breadcrumbs to tighten the mix,

and then I thought about the final ingredient that Jeff had instructed us to add: a little bit of love.

As I worked on the peppers on the morning of the funeral I couldn't help but think about the first couple of times I had tried my hand at preparing them. Immediately after receiving the recipe, I prepared a batch with a watering mouth, imagining that I would now be able to create the same peppers that I'd tasted at every gathering. It didn't quite work out that way. Even though I had the recipe, I didn't quite get it right. The peppers were okay, but they weren't quite there. Perhaps I'd mixed up the ingredients somehow, as they were blah compared to the ones Jeff normally made.

"You didn't tell me how much of everything to put in," I complained to Jeff.

"The love is the main ingredient, my stupid brother. You need to get that right to figure it out. Since you're making the peppers for just yourself to gorge on, perhaps you screwed it up."

I tried again a couple of weeks later, and I made another phone call. "I'm close with the peppers," I said.

"No, you're not," he answered.

A month later, I followed Kathy and the kids into the annual luau party thrown by Mike Livecchi and his wife Carla. Jeff had just entered carrying two trays of his stuffed hot peppers. He held the tray low enough for me to grab a couple of the peppers before he put them in the center of the table. I immediately stuffed them into my mouth, fearful that someone might steal them from me.

"You aren't even close, are you?" he asked. I just laughed. "Love, my man, love," Jeff said. "You don't have enough, and your probably don't wash your hands, either."

As I worked to core pepper after pepper, I had to keep moving the bowl containing the mixture to the side because the tears were falling with each pepper cored. The love that filled my heart was threatening an explosion of sorts, but I kept working.

"How did he do this every time?" I asked.

I prepared more than one hundred peppers and wrapped them in three pans to deliver to the reception that would follow the funeral.

At the funeral parlor I sat stone-faced as Jeff's family and friends gathered. I was holding Kathy's hand, but I kept removing it from her grasp to adjust the dark blue New York Yankee tie that belonged to Jeff. I didn't want to be wearing one of his ties at his funeral. It was the one place in the world where I never thought I'd be.

Mike Livecchi stood at the podium to say a few words before the priest's blessing at the funeral parlor. I considered the difficult task facing Mike, but he stood proud and offered a moving tribute to the man who'd shared his golf cart with him on so many days. Many of Mike's words were lost on me however, as pain threatened my heart and left me a quivering mess. Kathy through her own tear-stained eyes struggled to hold me up.

The priest offered a simple blessing, and the hundreds of people gathered headed for their cars in the parking lot. As I made my way toward my own car, I took comfort in the fact that Jeff's friends had covered hundreds of miles for the chance to say goodbye.

At the church I sat beside my parents, siblings, Lynn and the children. Behind us the church continued to fill up, and when the students from the Gow School, in full uniform, filed in, the struggle to find a decent breath of air was too much to take.

"Oh, Jesus," I cried and thankfully my sister Carrie wrapped her arms around my neck and squeezed me tightly. "I love you," she whispered.

The Mass of Christian burial began, and like zombies

we said the words to the prayers. The priest offered a stirring eulogy to Jeff and included a couple of his most famous pranks that provided the gathering with a much-needed laugh. As the priest concluded his message, Carrie turned to me. "Are you ready?" she asked.

I knew that there was no way that I could stand before the church filled with people and make sense of what was happening, but Carrie Lynn knew that we had to try. I followed Carrie to the lectern at the front of the church. She would perform the eulogy, and I would read the words to a Springsteen song, Terry's Song, in tribute to our brother.

"I don't know if I can handle this," I whispered to Carrie as we approached the lectern. My beautiful sister gripped my hand in support. "He would be mad if we didn't," she whispered.

From my spot behind Carrie, I could see the faces of Jeff's loved ones. The gathering was silent, as Carrie's words reached their ears. "In our grief, regret is not welcome. In our grief, our sadness moves us to grace. In our grief, there is no room for anger. In our grief, love prevails." Carrie's voice was loud and strong. The faces of my parents contorted in pain. Lynn's eyes showed the tremendous hurt felt by all.

"Love prevails," Carrie continued. "Love as the husband to Lynn. Love as the daddy to John, Farrah and Rocco. Love as the son of Mom and Dad. Love as the brother of Corinne, Chuck, John, Dana, Cliff, Kathy, Jim, Lisa and me. Love to Adam, Andrea, Matt, Nicole, Jake, James, Sam, Paige and Tony…their Uncle Bozo. Love to his aunts and uncles, cousins, his friends, his work. To the Town of North Collins…fun-loving, high-spirited, streaking clown of love."

There were a few chuckles as the people thought of Jeff as the 'streaking clown of love'. I felt myself spinning in a dizzying, confusing despair of realization. I was standing in front of the church, listening to my sister say goodbye. Why? Dear God, Why?

"He's right here in our hearts," Carrie continued. "And he'll be at the next Bruce concert; he'll be at the next Yankee game; he'll be at the dinner table for pasta on Sundays; he'll be cooking at Christmas; he'll be in the dandelion salad and the stuffed hot peppers; he'll be sticking his finger in your mouth whenever you yawn; he'll be dancing to the YMCA every single time that we hear it; he'll be wrapping his arms around the kids; he'll be in every ice sculpture; shooting hoops; swinging a bat; he'll be dipping a chew; he'll be drinking a beer, or two, or three."

An overwhelming sense of pride filled my heart. Carrie had been right about one thing: the only way through this was with love, and she was providing the guiding light for us to follow. Carrie concluded her brilliant words, and turned to face me. "Be strong," she whispered.

A momentary panic was quickly replaced by the thought that I needed to share the words of the Spring- steen song to the very best of my abilities. I thought of Jeff being there for me, every single time throughout the course of his life. I considered what he meant to each person in that filled church, and I thought of how much he would want the world to know that his love would carry on. I stepped to the microphone after hugging Carrie, and I read through the words written by Springsteen but deep- ly felt by all that morning: "They say that you can't take it with you, but I say that they're wrong, all I know is I woke up this morning and something big was gone. When they built you, brother, they broke the mold."

I stepped from the lectern and my sister and I wrapped our arms around one another. "He'd be proud," Carrie whispered.

Despite the fact that we'd been forced to say goodbye

to Jeff, we all realized that there was no way to properly handle the task. We would forever search for Jeff's smile, his spirit and his companionship for the remainder of our lives. Our faith had reminded us to anticipate an eternity where we would share with Jeff once more. However, there was no summing it all up or putting a bow on an undeniably full life that had been cut tragically short. There was no way to fill that void created by the loss, but there was a certain consolation in knowing that we wouldn't have missed even a second of Jeff's time here and that he was as loved as much as a person can possibly be.

The ceremony concluded at the foot of Shirley Road in the cemetery at the beginning of the road where we grew to adults. Jeff's eternal resting place would be less than a mile from the house on the hill where we had shared our love. The final prayers at the grave were spoken through a brisk breeze, in cool temperatures. Our family was together, but we were certainly broken by what was happening. I placed my hand on Jeff's casket as sobs took hold of me and nearly dropped me to my knees. The loving hand of my wife held me up, and I offered my other hand to my inconsolable mother.

Stepping away from the grave marker I felt my brother John's hand on my shoulder. "We're going to miss him every three minutes from here on in," John said.

After the funeral, friends entered my parents home to express their love and to offer support. Friends of the family, long since moved away to other parts of the country, drove hundreds of miles to pay their respects. My college roommates from twenty years before drove through the night to be there for Jeff's funeral. When I hugged Jeff Taylor, Terry Hancock, Mike Palmer and Mike Gaglianone, I cried not out of sadness, but because they were there when I needed their love.

Each of my siblings and my parents received as much

support from their friends, but while unbelievably appreci-
ated, the book of thanks would be too massive for publi-
cation.

Another buddy, Aaron "Duke" DeCarlo, stayed for quite
awhile with the family following the funeral Mass. Despite
the fact that Aaron had lost his mother and father at a
young age, he had spent years developing a sense of
humor that played like a wonderful stand-up comedy act.
In the hours following the funeral, Aaron provided the gift
of laughter. In between jokes, he cried as hard as the rest
of us, but his love that afternoon was unbelievably appre-
ciated.

Of course, there were many beautiful words spoken
and long embraces held, but the hole in our hearts was
just beginning to show itself. We would need so much
love to fill the empty space. I honestly couldn't string
more than two coherent thoughts together. There were
so many people hurting, and there was so much to do,
but it was all just so unacceptable. I didn't want people
to console me. I didn't want them to ask me if "I remem-
bered when." Instead, I just wanted to curl up into a ball
and sleep. I just wanted to see how long I could sleep.
Yet the horrific reality of suffering such a loss is that sleep
doesn't come easily, and when it does, it is at best fit-
ful and not at all refreshing. There are certainly no other
thoughts allowed when first opening your eyes, and
morning after morning, I cried so deeply, feeling the hurt
from my hair to my toenails.

"Jeff wouldn't want us to be sad," I continued to say
over and over, but the understanding in my heart was that
joy would no longer be possible.

I read through a number of moving tributes offered by
family and friends. I cried through tributes by people who
I barely knew anymore.

Tears streamed down my face as I thought of the pain

of our cousins, Jacqui Bollinger, the Switalas, the Gallegos, the Georges, Carol and Mike Wittmeyer, Tony, Wendy and Louie Fazzolari, Paul and Joe Bantle and dozens and dozens of others who offered support.

Friends who'd shared the walk with Jeff came from near and far to tell us story after story. Brad Gier made a plaque of the lyrics of Springsteen's Blood Brothers, and presented it to each of Jeff's siblings. He also shared a story that was pure Jeff.
***

The North Collins traveling hardball team comprised a group of tight friends who had joined forces simply to play the game of baseball, have a few beers and enjoy one another's companionship. The core of the team included Scott Hemer, Brad Gier, Tony Puntillo, Jeff Wolf, Jeff Ebersole and Jeff Fazzolari. The players on the team often rode together to games all across Western New York.

One cold and rainy Saturday morning in August, the players were stranded as the right rear tire on Jeff Ebersole's car was punctured and necessitated a quick change on a quiet road. Ebby pulled the car to the shoulder of the road, and in the driving rain, the men in the car formulated their plan.

The car was poised on a huge hill and there wasn't a single man who was excited about the prospect of getting soaking wet before the game. Scott Hemer took control of the situation.

"All right, Wolfie can jack up the car. Brad and I will loosen the lug nuts, and Ebby can grab the tire when we have it loose. Jeff, you'll get the spare and slap it on and Brad and I will tighten the lug nuts. It'll be like NASCAR. We'll change the flat in about six minutes."

The plan nearly worked. Wolfie jacked up the car; Scott and Brad, drenched by the rain that mixed with the mud, quickly removed the lug nuts. Ebby pulled the tire off, and all at once each man turned to Jeff to find out what was going on with the spare tire.

"Where's the spare?" Hemer called out.

"There it goes!" Jeff yelled out.

They all watched as the spare tire spun down the steep hill behind the car.

"Why would you do that?" Brad asked. "We need that tire."

"That's what makes it so funny," Jeff said as the tire rolled perfectly down the hill and circled to a stop, nearly a half-mile away.

***

It wasn't only Jeff's friends and family members who offered support in the days immediately following the ceremony. The Gow School community also wrapped the Fazzolari family in a warm embrace. In the days following the funeral, an article written by Jeff's co-worker, Julie Hadley, appeared in the East Aurora Advertiser. In the article, Julie related the story of the job interview she'd had with Jeff on the day that she was hired. Jeff had participated in the interview while wearing a wig and pretending that there wasn't anything amiss.

The kitchen in the new dining facility at the Gow School was also dedicated to Jeff's memory, and at a loving and moving ceremony, student after student cried right along with the faculty and our family. The dizzying tributes paid perfect testament to a life lived right, but there was just so much pain to consider. The pain that each one of us was feeling was bound to take up permanent residence in our hearts.

Through the years we've all muttered that the world will keep on spinning no matter what else is going on, and I suppose it is true. It's certainly cruel, but undeniably true.

Lynn and the kids were, of course, caught in a whirlwind of deep emotional pain that threatened them every moment. It was evident that the entire family would need time to heal, but the clock was still ticking. Life was still moving. Everyday tasks such as eating, and playing and getting up and out of bed needed to be handled. But the pain always crouched in the shadows, waiting for a chance to attack.

"The kids are coming by on Saturday," Kathy said one afternoon just a week following the funeral. "We can watch them all for awhile, right?"

"Absolutely," I said, but my heart was in my throat and my voice cracked with emotion. "Any time, all the time."

In my heart, however, I was dreading see Johnny, Farrah and Rocco. It wasn't because I was selfishly feeling my own hurt, but because I did not want to see even a hint of sadness in their eyes.

The car pulled to the curb early on Saturday and Lynn led the parade of kids to our front door. I stifled a sob that was building deep inside and put on my best "Uncle Cliff" face.

A funny thing happened when the kids saw me standing in the doorway. It's so easy to put adult things on children's heads, but they can't help but carry a grace into any given situation. Rocco ran toward me with his arms outstretched and I pulled him up quickly. He grabbed for my nose and I twisted out of the way, feigning disgust. Johnny headed straight by me, looking for his cousins, and Farrah sheepishly entered last, holding a toy in her hand.

"Come on in!" I yelled, surprised that my voice was so strong.

I looked into Lynn's eyes and she reflected my sadness right back to me. "I'll get them in a few hours," she said. "Is that okay?"

"Do whatever you need to do," I answered. "They can stay forever if you want."

Lynn thanked us and left. Even her walk was shrouded in utter sadness.

Of course the difficult part of losing someone that everyone loves is that all involved need to step through the stages of grief together, and that was extremely difficult given what we'd just been through. There was so much that should've been said at that time, but I had no way to put any coherent thoughts together. I know that we all wish that we could have done more for each other, but the hole in our own hearts was too massive.

For the next three hours we all played together in the backyard. I pushed Rocco on the swing; we chased the dogs around the backyard; and I did my best just to laugh with Jeff and Lynn's beautiful children, but soon enough, Johnny left the backyard and headed into the house.

"Where's Johnny?" I asked Kathy.

"He's up in your room alone," Kathy whispered. "He wanted to be by himself."

After some time, I headed toward my office. Seven-year old, Johnny was at my bookshelf, holding a copy of the book that I'd written about my son, Counting on a Miracle.

He dropped the book on the floor and scrambled away from the bookshelf as if I'd caught him doing something he wasn't supposed to do.

"Hey, buddy," I said.

"Did you write that?" he asked, pointing at the book.

"Yeah, that's about Jake," I said.

Johnny placed the book back on the shelf. He was looking at the floor, trying hard to avoid my eyes. My heart was beating so loudly that I was afraid it might scare him.

"Can you write a book about my dad?" he asked.

"Yeah, I'll do that if you want me to," I said.

"I do," Johnny said. "Because I'm really going to miss

him."

"Me too, buddy," I said.

Epilogue-Blood Brothers

From 1978 on, the New York Yankees were Jeff's first love. In the early '80s his favorite player was pitcher Dave Righetti, and for years he carried around the baseball card that chronicled Righetti's perfect game on the 4th of July. Jeff carried baseball cards in his wallet even after he reached 30!

Still there was no mistaking who Jeff's favorite all-time player was. Don Mattingly was the one true hero of those teams in the 80s and 90s, and it really didn't matter that the team was hardly ever in contention; the entire family shared an appreciation of how Mattingly played the game. I wish I had a dime for every time I walked into a room just to see Donnie Baseball bat. Jeff, to my knowledge, may have never missed an at-bat.

During those years, we four boys often sat out in the garage on a summer evening. Dad would prepare a cucumber and tomato salad, and we would eat, watch the Yanks and play cards. Night after wonderful summer night, we would listen to Frank White and Phil Rizzuto call the game.

Through the years there were also a number of trips to Toronto or Cleveland to see the Yankees play. One player, Dave Winfield, spent thirty minutes talking to Jeff after a Yankee victory over the Indians, and through his adult years, on any given day, Jeff's first thought of the day was about how the Yankees did the night before.

In 2000, the New York Yankees won the World Series over the New York Mets in a series that caused waves of excitement in New York City and throughout the Fazzolari family. On the day following the Yankees' victory in that series, Jeff called me early in the morning. We talked for well over an hour, giddy with excitement over what had transpired on the field the night before. It was the Yankees' third straight World Series championship and on that morning, there wasn't an end in sight. We believed, in our hearts, that they might reel off ten in a row. Yet it was not to be.

In 2001, the Yankees lost on the final play of the year, and witnessing the Yankees 27th championship would have to wait, and wait, and wait and wait. In an effort to end the drought, the Yankees signed a player from Japan, Hideki Matsui. It was a much anticipated signing that came with all of the usual fanfare. Matsui had a reputation as a real masher, and we dreamed of fifty or sixty homerun seasons as he brought the Yankees back to the Promised Land. Matsui's nickname was Godzilla, but a few games into the 2003 season it became apparent that he was more of a line-drive hitter whose power would not translate in the major league game. Matsui became a favorite target of Jeff's. "He isn't a homerun hitter. He's all right, but if he's Godzilla then I'm Mickey Mantle."

As a family, we all stood up for Matsui. Dad would insist that Matsui was a good ballplayer, but Jeff would have nothing of it. Of course he was still rooting for the Japanese import to do well, but he always voiced his displeasure.

One day in the middle of the '06 season, the telephone rang and I was pleasantly surprised to hear my nephew Johnny on the other end of the line. Johnny was 4-years-old and had just started to use the telephone on a coherent basis.

"Hi, Uncle Cliffy," he said.

"Hey, Johnny, what're you doing?"

I heard Jeff whisper something in the background.

"Matsui's a @$&*#$%&*," Johnny said.

"What?" I said.

Johnny said it again, and Jeff roared in the background.

Jeff took the phone from his young son.

"Are you out of your mind?" I asked.

Jeff was laughing uncontrollably.

"You can't teach him those words," I said.

"He won't remember," Jeff said.

Yet Jeff's cheeky prank was something that everyone in the family recalled on the night of November 4, 2009, as the Yankees prepared to clinch the title for the first time since 2000.

Preparing for the game, I couldn't help but curse the fact that I was going to be celebrating a championship without my best buddy. I was so conflicted that I was near tears when the game started, but something strange had happened earlier in the day. Feeling the incredible loss of not having Jeff around was too much to handle. So, before the game, on my Facebook page, I boldly declared that the Yanks would win and that Matsui would go deep. I didn't have to mention that Matsui was doing it in honor of Jeff. Everyone who ever met Jeff understood why I had made such a prediction.

Prior to the game, Sam, who owns a shirt of every Yankee player, entered the living room.

"Who are you wearing tonight?" I asked.

Sam spun around to show me the name on the back of his shirt: Matsui.

"Why did you choose him?" I asked.

Sam shrugged. "It was the first one I grabbed."

My eyes threatened tears, but I remained quiet.

The game was still scoreless when Matsui strolled to the plate for the first time. There was a runner on base, but there were two outs. Suddenly, my cell phone vibrated to announce that I had a text message.

"Matsui sucks," was the two-word message from Lynn.

On the very next pitch Matsui hit an upper-deck home-run to right.

"He just homered!" I texted back.

"He still sucks," was Lynn's perfect answer.

Little did she know that I was crying. How could she possibly know that when that ball landed, I felt as if Jeff were speaking right to me?

Yet the night was not over by any stretch of the imagination. Everyone in the family was sharing the moment: "Matsui's a @$&*#$%&*" was mentioned a hundred times.

In total, Matsui drove in six runs and won the MVP for the series. It was a World Series victory that I was certain that Jeff couldn't celebrate with us. Yet as the champagne flowed and as Matsui took to the podium, something told me that we were wrong. Jeff was right there with us.

In the days, and then weeks immediately following the Yankees clinching the win in the World Series, I continued to work hard to try to condition my mind to the fact that Jeff was gone. I knew that death was simply an extension of life, but a world that had once been filled with color seemed somehow black and white. Knowing that I needed to accept his death and actually accepting it were two entirely different matters.

Just a week before Thanksgiving in 2009, I lay in bed watching television. As had happened so many times during the year, I found that I wasn't following the action on the screen so well. The repeat of Seinfeld failed to hold my attention, and I found myself thinking back to a day much earlier in the year.

On that day, I hadn't wanted to be anywhere near Albany, New York. I was in town on business, but my thought the entire day was to get out of town, and get home. I was tired of trying to chase the pain away. I was sick of pretending that I was doing okay, and that my job mattered, or that the everyday words of those I met actually meant anything to me. I called Kathy, who was home, too far away from me to help me through the pain.

"Don't count on me until about ten tonight," I said. "The company wants me to visit a couple of their sites."

"I was just going to call you," Kathy said, "to tell you not to come home at all."

"What are you talking about?" I asked.

"You're in Albany, right?"

"Yeah, and it's going to take me five hours to get home."

"Don't bother. Bruce Springsteen is in Albany tonight!"

"Come on," I said.

"I swear, check it out."

The excitement of it all was enough to propel me to the arena where I was able to quickly buy a single seat, on the first level, not very far from the stage. I immediately called Kathy with the news.

"I got a ticket!"

"Good, enjoy life, right?"

The thought of Jeff sent a shiver of pain through my beaten-down heart. "You know, I don't think I can watch Bruce and be happy," I said.

"You can," Kathy said. "You were meant to see him by yourself right now."

An hour before the show was slated to begin, I sat in the parking lot at the motel. I was listening to Badlands, but the volume was down way low. "Jeff's not here," I cried. "He's the guy I want to call to tell him I'm seeing Bruce, and he's not here!"

The realization that Jeff was gone was paralyzing. "I can't go," I cried. "I can't fucking go!"

My ringing cell phone made the words catch in my throat. The screen flashed the name: Duke.

"Hey, buddy," Duke said. "Just checking in on you." I

cried out. "Are you okay?"

"I'm in Albany," I said. "Springsteen's here. I'm on my way to the show, but I can't do it. Jeff's gone, Duke. He's gone!"

"He's not gone," Duke said. "He'll never be gone, buddy. My mom and dad died years ago, but they're with me every minute of every day. Death can't separate you guys. Talk to Jeffrey and sing to him. He's going to be sitting right beside you."

I'm not certain that I would have made my way into the arena that night if it hadn't been for Duke's perfectly timed telephone call. Bruce took the stage to wild cheers, but I wasn't cheering, I was crying.

"I know that some of you are sad! I know that some of you are broken-hearted," Bruce cried out in a preacher-like tone. "Tonight I'm here to take away a little of the pain! Tonight our job is to make you smile!"

I tipped my Yankee cap to the rafters.

As the concert wound down some three hours later, I was sure that I was done crying. Bruce and the E Street Band exited the stage, and I turned to the virtual stranger sitting in the seat beside me.

"They're done," the guy announced.

"They're going to do one more song," I said.

"I don't think so," he said, but the words were no sooner out of his mouth when the lights dimmed again.

"They can't leave without playing my brother's favorite song," I said. "American Land."

As if he knew what I was going through, Springsteen led the band through the opening riff.

I am certain of one thing. I sang the song louder than Bruce did that night.

***

Months later, as I drifted toward sleep on that cold November night, I considered celebrating the Yankees win without Jeff. I thought of attending the Springsteen concert alone, and I struggled with the ridiculous notion that I would eventually have to accept that fact that Jeff was physically gone from my life.

Of course, I don't remember the moment when I lapsed into the dream, but it soon filled my sleep, and the dream was so vivid that I couldn't help but feel that I wasn't dreaming at all.

"I'm all right," Jeff said. He was standing at the side of my bed in full health. There was a Yankee World Series hat on his head and he was smiling.

"You're not all right," I said. "You're gone."

"I'm telling you I'm all right, pumpkin. I'm right here. Now come on, I got Springsteen tickets. They're in the second row. You paid for them."

We found our seats just mere feet away from Springsteen. Jeff was wearing a bright red fleece pullover sweatshirt with the Yankee cap. He was holding a beer in his right hand and his left was draped over my shoulder. Bruce was on stage, screaming the words of Outlaw Pete, the very last song that Jeff would ever hear.

"Can you hear me?" Springsteen cried out.

"Can you hear me?" Jeff echoed.

The dream continued outside the arena where Jeff stopped to take a quick leak behind the Dumpster.

"I told you to minimize your chances of getting in trouble," I scolded.

"A-ha-a-ha-a-ha-a-ha-a-ha," Jeff replied. "And I told you to enjoy life." Jeff finished his task and jogged to catch up to the spot by my side as we walked toward our car in the parking lot.

"I can't enjoy life if you aren't here," I said.

"I am right here, my brother," he said. "I'll always be right next to you. I'm in the air you breathe. I'm always ready to tickle you."

I turned quickly to avoid the tickle, and when I glanced sideways, he was gone. The space to my right was empty, and he'd left without saying goodbye.

I didn't bolt upright in the bed with the realization that Jeff was gone and that the dream was over. Instead, I took a deep breath and settled into the warm embrace of the comforter. Jeff was all right. He'd told me himself. He hadn't needed to say goodbye because he never really left. All through his life he'd hung up without saying good-bye because he knew that he'd be talking with me again soon. He was at peace. I needed to be, too. I slipped back into sleep, hoping that somehow I could continue working on the dream.

Acknowledgements

Love surely knows no bounds. Despite the tragic loss of Jeff, there is hope alive because of the love that surrounds our family. Acknowledging all who helped in the creation of this book would take more space than I have here. It would be wonderful to list each name, and I hope you made it into some of the stories that were part of a truly loving life.

To our hundreds and hundreds of friends, I'll never get tired of saying thank you, and we wouldn't have made it through the funeral without you bringing the love.

A special thank you is extended to the Gow School, where Jeff worked as an executive chef. Your generosity of spirit is appreciated.

During the course of writing this book, the Fazzolari family suffered another horrific loss as our other leader, John Fazzolari, passed away in August of 2010. Dad never quite got used to the idea that Jeff was no longer just a telephone call away, and now, we all know that they are together again. Dad and Jeff are laughing, sharing and loving as they always did.

To the extended Fazzolari family, and all of our great friends and relatives, we are still living the dream, and Jeff and Dad are still providing the heartbeat.

Author's Notes

The stories contained in this book are told through the voice of the author, but facts and memories were gathered through the years.

The contributions of family members are noted and appreciated more than you'll ever know. There isn't a doubt in my mind that each and every one of us could have written a book of stories.

This was a difficult chore but only because there were way too many stories to recall. Every single moment of his roughly 13,394 days was an event that could have been chronicled.

Jeff had a true zest for life, and I just know that as I wrote, he was in the chair beside me, chiding me to get it right, and for God's sake, make it funny.

In the end, I can only pray that I did him proud because he made each and every one of us proud to walk beside him.

clifford fc @ roadrunner